American Headway 1B

THE WORLD'S MOST TRUSTED ENGLISH COURSE

Youngseok Alex Kim

SECOND EDITION

Liz and John Soars

OXFORD
UNIVERSITY PRESS

Scope and Sequence

Grammar: Past Simple 1 – Regular verbs • Irregular verbs
Vocabulary: Words that go together
Everyday English: What's the date?

STARTER When were your grandparents and great-grandparents born? Where were they born? Do you know all their names? What were their jobs? If you know, tell the class.

A life past and present
Past Simple – regular verbs

1 Look at the photos. Do you know anything about the TV star, Oprah Winfrey?

2 `CD2 20` Read and listen to Oprah Winfrey's life now. Complete Text **A** with the verbs you hear. Answer the questions.

1. How many people watch her show?
2. Where does she live?
3. Does she earn a lot of money?

3 `CD2 21` Read and listen to Text **B** about Oprah's childhood. Answer the questions.

1. Where and when was she born?
2. Were her parents rich?
3. Was she smart? What could she do?

GRAMMAR SPOT

1 Complete the sentences about Oprah.

Now she _____ in California.
When she was a child she _____ with her grandmother.

2 Look at Text **B**. Find the Past Simple of the verbs *work*, *clean*, *receive*, *study*, and *start*. How is it formed?

▶▶ **Grammar Reference 7.1 p. 118**

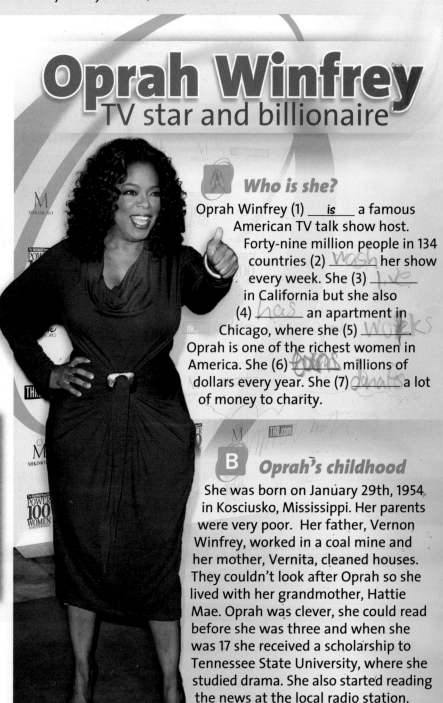

Oprah Winfrey
TV star and billionaire

A Who is she?

Oprah Winfrey (1) __is__ a famous American TV talk show host. Forty-nine million people in 134 countries (2) _wash_ her show every week. She (3) _live_ in California but she also (4) _has_ an apartment in Chicago, where she (5) _works_. Oprah is one of the richest women in America. She (6) _earns_ millions of dollars every year. She (7) _donates_ a lot of money to charity.

B Oprah's childhood

She was born on January 29th, 1954 in Kosciusko, Mississippi. Her parents were very poor. Her father, Vernon Winfrey, worked in a coal mine and her mother, Vernita, cleaned houses. They couldn't look after Oprah so she lived with her grandmother, Hattie Mae. Oprah was clever, she could read before she was three and when she was 17 she received a scholarship to Tennessee State University, where she studied drama. She also started reading the news at the local radio station.

C Oprah the TV star

In 1984 Oprah (1) _moved_ to Chicago to work on a TV talk show called *A.M. Chicago*. She (2) _talked_ to lots of interesting people about their problems. Oprah says, "People's problems are my problems." The show was very successful, so in 1985 it was renamed *The Oprah Winfrey Show*. In 1993 she (3) _interviewed_ Michael Jackson and 100 million people (4) _watched_ the program. Last year she (5) _earned_ $260,000,000.

In 1998 Oprah (6) _started_ the charity Oprah's Angel Network. This helps poor children all over the world. In 2007 she (7) _opened_ a special school in South Africa, the Oprah Winfrey Leadership Academy for Girls. She says, "When I was a kid, we were poor and we didn't have much money. So what did I do? I (8) _studied_ hard." There are 152 girls at the school. Oprah calls them her daughters— the children she didn't have in real life.

---

4 **CD2 22** What is the past of these verbs? Listen and repeat.

watch	talk	move	interview
earn	open	study	start

5 **CD2 23** Listen to Text **C**. Complete it with the past form of the verbs in Exercise 4.

GRAMMAR SPOT

1 Look at these questions. Which are present? Which are past?

"Where does Oprah work?"
"In Chicago."

"Where did her father work?"
"In a coal mine."

"Did she have a happy childhood?"
"No, she didn't."

"Does she have any children?"
"No, she doesn't."

➤ *Did* is the past of *do* and *does*.

2 We use *didn't* (= *did not*) to form the negative.

We **didn't** have much money.

3 Find a question and two negatives in Text **C**.

▶▶ **Grammar Reference 7.2 p. 118**

6 Complete the questions about Oprah.
1. Where __did__ her father __work__?
   In a coal mine.
2. What _did_ her mother do?
   She cleaned houses.
3. Who _did_ Oprah _lived_ with?
   Her grandmother.
4. What _did_ she _studied_? Drama.
5. When _did_ she _interviewed_ Michael Jackson?
   In 1993.
6. How much _did_ she _earned_ last year?
   $260 million.
7. When _did_ she _opened_ the girls school?
   In 2007.
8. _Did_ her parent _earn_ much money?
   No, they didn't.

CD2 24 Listen and check. Practice the questions and answers with a partner.

PRACTICE
Talking about you

1 Complete the sentences with *did*, *was*, or *were*.

1. Where _were_ you born?
   Where _was_ your mother born?
2. When _did_ you start school?
3. When _did_ you learn to read and write?
4. Who _was_ your first teacher?
5. What _was_ your favorite subject?
6. Where _did_ you live when you _were_ a child?
7. _did_ you live in a house or an apartment?

2 Stand up! Ask two or three students the questions in Exercise 1.

3 Tell the class some of the information you learned.

Rick was born in ...

His mother ...

He started school ...

Pronunciation

1 **CD2 25** Listen to three different pronunciations of *-ed*.

/t/	/d/	/ɪd/
worked	lived	started

2 **CD2 26** Listen and write the Past Simple verbs in the correct column.

/t/	/d/	/ɪd/

Practice saying them.

THE YEAR I WAS BORN
Irregular verbs

1 Look at the list of irregular verbs on page 133. Write the Past Simple form of the verbs in the box. Which verb isn't irregular?

be	_was/were_	beat	_beat_	become	_became_	begin	_began_
buy	_bought_	come	_came_	get	_got_	go	_went_
have	_had_	hit	_hit_	invent	_invented_	leave	_leaved_
make	_made_	sell	_seled_	sing	_sang_	win	_wond_

2 **CD2 27** Listen and repeat the Past Simple forms.

3 James was born in 1989. Look at the pictures. What things from 1989 can you see?

4 **CD2 28** Listen to James's conversation with his parents about 1989. Complete the sentences with the verbs you hear. Listen again and check.

1989 ... the year I was born

James was born on January 24, 1989, in São Paulo, where his father (1) _had_ a job. His parents (2) _left_ Brazil that year and (3) _went back_ back to the U.S. His father (4) _got_ a job in New York.

WORLD EVENTS
In the U.S., George Herbert Walker Bush (5) _became_ the 41st American President. In Russia, Mikhail S. Gorbachev (6) _began_ the Soviet Head of State. In Europe, the Cold War between East and West ended and, after 28 years, the Berlin Wall (7) _came_ down.

SPORTS
In Major League Baseball, the Oakland Athletics (8) _beat_ the San Francisco Giants in the World Series. The Series stopped for twelve days when a major earthquake (9) _hit_ the San Francisco Bay Area moments before the start of Game Three.

SCIENCE/TECHNOLOGY
Tim Berners-Lee (10) _invented_ the World Wide Web. He (11) _won_ many awards and $1.5 million. Nintendo (12) _began_ selling Game Boy in Japan. They (13) _sold_ 30 million in three years.

ENTERTAINMENT
The Simpsons family (14) _made_ their television debut. Madonna (15) _sang_ "Like a Prayer." It was a number one hit. Twelve million people (16) _bought_ the album.

5 Work with a partner. Ask and answer questions about the year James was born.

1. When/James and his parents leave Brazil?
2. Where/his father get a job?
3. How many years/the Berlin Wall stand?
4. Why/the baseball game stop?
5. What/Tim Berners-Lee invent?
6. How much money/he win?
7. How many Game Boys/Nintendo sell?
8. What/Madonna sing?

6 What happened the year you were born? Write some notes. Tell the class.

PRACTICE

When did it happen?

1 Work in groups. Think of important events in history. When did they happen? Make a list, then make questions to ask the other groups.

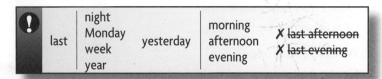

> When did the Second World War begin/end?

> When did the first person walk on the moon?

What did you do?

!	last	night Monday week year	yesterday	morning afternoon evening	✗ last afternoon ✗ last evening

2 Work with a partner. Ask and answer questions with *When did you last … ?* Ask another question for more information.

> When did you last take a vacation?

> Last August.

> Where did you go?

> To Florida.

- take a vacation
- watch a DVD
- go shopping
- take a photograph
- go to a party
- talk on a cell phone
- write an e-mail
- get a present
- eat in a restaurant

Tell the class some things you learned about your partner.

> Yukio took a vacation last August and she went to Italy.

Check it

3 Put a check (✓) next to the correct sentence.

1. ☑ He bought some new shoes.
   ☐ He buyed some new shoes.
2. ☑ Where did you go yesterday?
   ☐ Where you went yesterday?
3. ☐ You see Jane last week?
   ☑ Did you see Jane last week?
4. ☑ Did she get the job?
   ☑ Did she got the job?
5. ☑ I went out yesterday night.
   ☑ I went out last night.
6. ☑ He studied French at school.
   ☐ He studyed French at school.
7. ☐ What had you for breakfast?
   ☑ What did you have for breakfast?
8. ☐ I was in New York the last week.
   ☑ I was in New York last week.

▶▶ **WRITING** Describing a vacation *p. 98*

READING AND SPEAKING
Two famous firsts

Two

1 Translate these words.

nouns	verbs	adjectives
airshow	break a record	excellent
fighter jet	travel	dangerous
flight	disappear	secret
experiences	join	
satellite	survive	
	crash	

2 Look at the texts and complete these sentences.

Amelia Mary Earhart was the first _____ .

Yuri Gagarin was the first _____ .

3 Work in two groups.

Group A Read about Amelia Earhart.
Group B Read about Yuri Gagarin.

4 Are the sentences true (✓) or false (✗) about your person?
Correct the false sentences.

1. ___✗___ He/She came from a rich family.
2. _____ He/She had a short but exciting life.
3. ___✗___ He/She fought in a World War.
4. ___✗___ He/She wanted to be a pilot when he/she was a child.
5. ___✗___ He/She flew fighter jets.
6. ___✗___ He/She married, but didn't have any children.
7. ___✓___ He/She traveled around the world to talk about his/her experiences.
8. ___✓___ He/She died in a plane crash.

5 Find a partner from the other group. Compare Amelia Earhart and Yuri Gagarin, using your answers.

6 Complete the questions about the other person. Then ask and answer them with your partner.

About Amelia Earhart
1. Where . . . she born?
2. What . . . she study first?
3. When . . . she first . . . up in a plane?
4. When . . . she . . . her first record?
5. . . . she marry? . . . she . . . any children?
6. What . . . she do in 1935?
7. Where . . . her plane disappear?

About Yuri Gagarin
8. Where . . . he born?
9. When . . . he see his first plane?
10. Why . . . he . . . the Russian Air Force?
11. Why . . . the doctors choose Yuri to be an astronaut?
12. What . . . he do in 1961?
13. Why . . . he . . . around the world?
14. How . . . he die?

What do you think?

Name some famous people from history. What did they do?

famous firsts

Amelia Mary Earhart AMERICAN (1897 – 1937)

The first woman to fly across the Atlantic

Her early years

Amelia was born in her grandparents' house in Kansas. Her parents didn't have any money, but her grandparents were rich and sent her to the best schools. At 20 she decided to study nursing and worked in a hospital in World War I. When she was 23, she visited an airshow and went up in a plane. At that moment, she knew that she wanted to be a pilot.

What she did

In 1920 flying was dangerous and people didn't think it was an activity for women. But Amelia took flying lessons, and a year later, she broke her first record — she flew up to 14,000 feet. She married at 34, but never had children. The next year she became the first woman (and the second person) to fly alone across the Atlantic. She was now famous, and she traveled around the world to talk about her experiences. And in 1935, when she was 38, she became the first person to fly alone across the Pacific.

Her last flight

When she was nearly 40, Amelia wanted to be the first woman to fly around the world. She began the 29,000 mile flight in Miami on June 1, 1937. On July 2 she was nearly at the end of her journey, when she and her plane disappeared near Howland Island in the Pacific Ocean.

Yuri Gagarin RUSSIAN (1934 – 1968)

The first man in space

His early years

Yuri was born on a farm and his family was very poor. As a teenager in World War II, he saw his first plane — a Russian fighter jet. At that moment, he knew that he wanted to be a pilot. He studied hard so that he could join a flying club. His teachers thought he was a natural pilot and told him to join the Russian Air Force.

What he did

He became an excellent pilot. And he was now a husband and father. But when the first Russian satellite went into space, he wanted to become an astronaut. After two years of secret training, the doctors chose Yuri because he was the best in all the tests. On April 12, 1961, when he was 27, he finally went into space. It was very dangerous, because the doctors didn't know if Yuri could survive the journey. When he came back to Earth he was famous, and he traveled around the world to talk about his experiences.

His last flight

He wanted to go into space again, so in 1967 he began training for the next space flight. He was also a test pilot for new Air Force airplanes. But the next year he died when his fighter jet crashed on a test flight. He was only 34.

VOCABULARY AND LISTENING
Words that go together

Verbs and nouns

1 Match a verb in **A** with a noun in **B**.
Sometimes there is more than one answer.

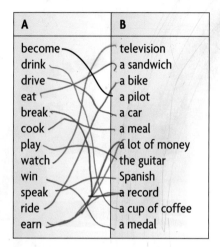

A	B
become	television
drink	a sandwich
drive	a bike
eat	a pilot
break	a car
cook	a meal
play	a lot of money
watch	the guitar
win	Spanish
speak	a record
ride	a cup of coffee
earn	a medal

Ask and answer questions.

> Do you drink tea in the morning?

> No, I don't. I drink coffee.

> When did you last eat a sandwich?

> This morning./Yesterday./Last week.

Prepositions

2 Complete the sentences with the correct preposition.

1. I like listening ___to___ music.
2. I went ___To___ the beach ___with___ my friends.
3. We went to Jamaica ___on___ our vacation last year.
4. She traveled ___around___ the world.
5. I get up ___At___ eleven o'clock ___on___ Sundays.
6. My father works ___in___ an office downtown.
7. Our town has a lot ___of___ tourists ___in___ the summer.
8. My parents are ___at___ home ___at___ the moment.
9. What's ___on___ television this evening?
10. I wrote an e-mail ___to___ my daughter.

Compound nouns

3 Match a noun in **A** with a noun in **B**.
Do we write one word or two?

post office   homework

A	B
orange	paper
train	room
swimming	pool
hand	juice
boy	lot
news	star
movie	card
birthday	station
washing	machine
living	friend
parking	bag

CD2 29 Listen, check, and repeat.

4 Test the other students!

> This is where we can go swimming.

> A swimming pool!

> I buy this every day and read it.

> A newspaper.

5 **CD2 30** Listen to four conversations. What are they about? Which compound nouns do you hear?

1. hand bag
2. chocolat cake
3. boy friend
4. poste offer

Look at the audio script on page 108.
Practice the four conversations with a partner.

EVERYDAY ENGLISH
What's the date?

1 Write the correct word below the numbers.

fourth	twelfth	sixth	twentieth	second	thirtieth
thirteenth	thirty-first	fifth	seventeenth	tenth	
sixteenth	first	third	twenty-first		

1st **2nd** **3rd** **4th** **5th**

first second third fourth fifth

6th **10th** **12th** **13th** **16th**

sixth tenth twenth thidem sixteenth

17th **20th** **21st** **30th** **31st**

seventeenth tweny thidet thirteen
twenton fist

CD2 31 Listen and practice saying the ordinals.

2 Ask and answer questions with a partner about the months of the year.

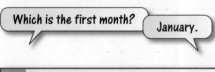
Which is the first month?

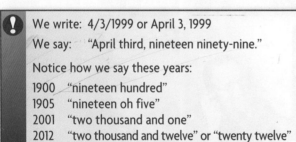
January.

> ! We write: 4/3/1999 or April 3, 1999
>
> We say: "April third, nineteen ninety-nine."
>
> Notice how we say these years:
>
> 1900 "nineteen hundred"
> 1905 "nineteen oh five"
> 2001 "two thousand and one"
> 2012 "two thousand and twelve" or "twenty twelve"

3 Practice saying these dates.

April 1   November 19   12/19/83

March 2   June 23   10/3/99

September 17   2/29/76   5/31/2000

7/15/2007

CD2 32 Listen and check.

4 **CD2 33** Listen and write the dates you hear.

5 Ask and answer the questions with your partner.

1. What's the date today?
2. When did this class start? When does it end?
3. When's Valentine's Day?
4. When's Mother's Day this year?
5. When's your birthday?
6. What century is it now?
7. What are the dates of public holidays in your country?

STARTER   What is the Past Simple of these verbs? Most of them are irregular.

> eat   drink   drive   fly   listen to   make   ride   take   watch   wear

FAMOUS INVENTIONS
Past Simple negatives – *ago*

1 Match the verbs from the Starter with the photos.

2 Work in groups. What year was it a hundred years ago? Ask and answer questions about the things in the photos. What did people do? What didn't they do?

> Did people drive cars a hundred years ago?

> Yes, I think they did.

> I'm not so sure.

> No, they didn't.

3 Tell the class the things you think people did and didn't do.

> We think people drove cars, but they didn't watch TV.

Getting information

4 When were the things in the photos invented? Ask and answer with a partner.

Student A   Go to page 124.
Student B   Go to page 125.

> **A** When were cars invented?
> **B** In ... .
> **A** That's ... years ago.

1 **watch**   television

2 drink   Coca-Cola

3 make   phone calls

4 drive   cars

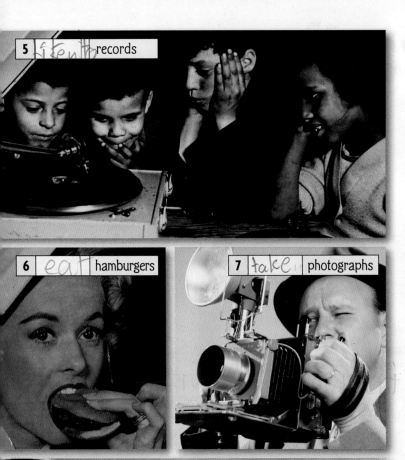

5 [listenth] records

6 [eat] hamburgers

7 [take] photographs

8 [Fly] planes

9 [ride] bikes

BLUE BELL WRANGLERS
are a family affair!

10 [wear] jeans

1 Write the Past Simple forms.

Present Simple	Past Simple
I live in Seattle.	I lived in Seattle.
He lives in Seattle.	He lived in Seattle
Do you live in Seattle?	did you live in Seattle
Does she live in Seattle?	dis she lived in seatl
I don't live in Seattle.	I did not live in
He doesn't live in Seattle.	H does not lived in Seattle

2 Complete these sentences.

The year 2000 was ___16___ years ago.

The year 1984 was ___32___ years ago.

▶▶ **Grammar Reference 8.1 and 8.2 p. 118**

PRACTICE

Time expressions

1 Make correct time expressions.

in
on
at

at seven o'clock	in the morning
on Saturday	on Sunday evening
at night	in September
in 2002	on weekends
in the summer	in the nineteenth century

2 Work with a partner. Ask and answer questions with *When … ?* Use a time expression and *ago* in the answer.

> **When did you get up?**
>> At seven o'clock, three hours ago.

> **When did this semester start?**
>> In September, two months ago.

When did … ?

- you get up
- you have breakfast
- you arrive at school
- you start learning English
- you start at this school
- this semester start
- you last use a computer
- you learn to ride a bicycle
- your parents get married
- you last have a coffee break

3 Tell the class about your day so far. Begin like this.

I got up at seven o'clock and had breakfast. I left the house at …

PRACTICE

Three inventions

1 Look at the texts. What are the three inventions?

2 **CD2 34** The dates in the texts are *all* incorrect. Read and listen, and correct the dates.

> Daguerre didn't start his experiments in the 1920s. He started them in the 1820s.

3 Make these sentences negative. Then give the correct answers.
1. Daguerre invented the bicycle.
   He didn't invent the bicycle.
   He invented the photograph.
2. Daguerre gave his idea to the French government.
3. Mary Anderson lived in New York City.
4. All cars had windshield wipers by 1916.
5. Leonardo da Vinci made the first bicycle.
6. Kirkpatrick Macmillan came from France.

CD2 35 Listen and check. Practice the stress and intonation.

4 Work with a partner. Make more incorrect sentences about the texts. Give them to a partner to correct.

Did you know that?

5 **CD2 36** Read and listen to the conversations. Then listen and repeat.

> **A** Did you know that Marco Polo brought spaghetti back from China?
> **B** Really? That's incredible!
> **A** Well, it's true!
>
> **C** Did you know that Napoleon was afraid of cats?
> **D** No way! I don't believe it!
> **C** Well, it's true!

6 Work with a partner.
Student A Go to page 124.
Student B Go to page 126.
Make similar conversations.

The photograph
LOUIS DAGUERRE FROM FRANCE

Louis Daguerre was a painter for the French opera. But he wanted to make a new type of picture. He started his experiments in the 1920s. Twelve years later he invented the photograph. He sold his idea to the French government in 1935 and the government gave it to the world. Daguerre called the first photographs "daguerreotypes." They became popular very fast. By 1940, there were 70 daguerreotype studios in New York City.

The bicycle
KIRKPATRICK MACMILLAN FROM SCOTLAND

Long ago in 1540, Leonardo da Vinci drew a design for the modern bicycle. But the first person to make a bicycle was Kirkpatrick Macmillan in 1789. He lived in Scotland, so people didn't hear about his invention for a long time. Twenty years later, another bicycle came from France. In 1825 the bike became cheap and everyone could have one. Now people, especially women, could travel to the next town. It helped them find someone to marry!

2

The windshield wiper

MARY ANDERSON FROM THE UNITED STATES

Mary Anderson often visited New York City by car. In winter she noticed that when it rained or snowed, drivers got out of their cars all the time to clean their windows. In 1893 she began designing something to clean windows from inside the car. People, especially men, laughed at her idea. But they didn't laugh for long. She invented the windshield wiper in 1925. And by 1960 all American cars had them.

1 There are many silent letters in English words. Practice saying these words.

> know /noʊ/
> talk /tɔk/
> thought /θɔt/

Cross out the silent letters in these words.

1. walk	7. buy
2. listen	8. hour
3. widow	9. flight
4. write	10. could
5. eight	11. wrong
6. island	12. daughter

CD2 37 Listen and check. Practice saying the words.

2 Look at the phonetic spelling of these words from Exercise 1. Write the words.

1. /wɔk/ — **walk**
2. /baɪ/ — _____
3. /ˈlɪsən/ — _____
4. /wɪdoʊ/ — _____
5. /raɪt/ — _____
6. /aɪlənd/ — _____

3 Write the words. They all have silent letters.

1. /waɪt/ — **white**
2. /bɔt/ — _____
3. /naɪt/ — _____
4. /ˈɑænsər/ — _____
5. /bɪldɪŋ/ — _____
6. /ˈkrɪsməs/ — _____

CD2 38 Listen and practice saying the words.

4 Read these sentences aloud.

1. He bought his daughter eight white horses for Christmas.
2. I know you know the answer.
3. They walked and talked for hours and hours on the island.
4. Listen and answer the questions.
5. The girl took the wrong flight.

CD2 39 Listen and check.

▶▶ **Phonetic symbols** *p. 134*

LISTENING AND SPEAKING
How did you two meet?

1 Put the sentences in the correct order. There is more than one answer!

- 4 They got married.
- 2 They went out for a year.
- 3 They fell in love.
- 6 They had two children.
- 1 Jack and Jill met at a party.
- 5 They got engaged.

2 Look at the photos of two couples and read the introductions to their stories. What do you think happened next?

3 **CD2 40** Listen to them talking. Were your ideas correct?

4 Answer the questions about Neil and Claudia, and Eric and Lori.

1. Who was Stuart? Why didn't Claudia's friends like him?
2. What did Claudia's friends do?
3. Where did Eric and Lori's mothers meet?
4. Why didn't Eric and Lori want to meet?
5. Where did Neil first see Claudia?
6. What happened when both couples first met?
7. Which couple's wedding is next fall?

5 Who said these sentences? What was it about? Write **N**, **C**, **E**, or **L** in the boxes.

a. _L_ Our story is easy. We didn't do anything.
b. _C_ I didn't know anything about it!
c. _N_ I saw her picture and wrote to her.
d. _E_ I just thought, 'No way.'
e. _C_ Most of them went into my junk mailbox.
f. _E_ I took my sister with me.
g. _C_ ...immediately everything just clicked.
h. _E_ We all had a great time by the lake.

Speaking

6 Work with a partner. Imagine you are one of the people. Tell the story of how you met your boyfriend/girlfriend.

7 Look at these questions. Tell your partner about you and your family.

1. Are you married or do you have a girlfriend/ boyfriend? How did you meet?
2. When did your parents or grandparents meet? Where? How?

Neil
Claudia

He's not your type!

Sometimes our friends don't like the people we date. Claudia's friends didn't like her boyfriend, so she broke up with him. Her friends wanted her to have a new boyfriend, so they...

Eric
Lori

Do mothers know best?

Parents usually want their children to meet a nice person and get married. Eric's mom wanted to help him meet someone, so...

▶▶ **WRITING** About a friend *p. 99*

EVERYDAY ENGLISH
Special occasions

1 Look at the list of days. Which are special? Match the special days with the pictures.

birthday 1	yesterday 6	Easter
Mother's Day 5	Halloween 6	New Year's Eve 4
today	Monday	Valentine's Day 2
weekend	Thanksgiving	Friday
wedding day 3	tomorrow	Christmas Day 7

2 Which days do you celebrate in your country? What do you do?

- make a cake
- give cards and presents
- have a meal
- go out with friends
- wear special clothes
- watch fireworks
- have a party
- give flowers or chocolates

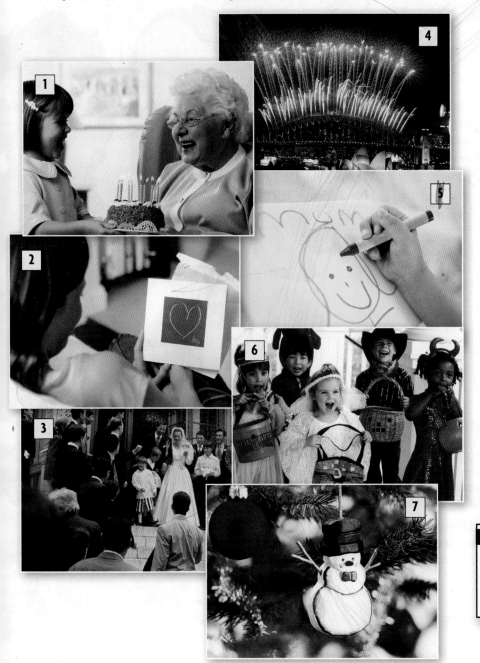

3 Complete the conversations. What are the occasions?

1. Happy _birthday_ to you.
   Happy _new year_ to you.
   Happy _mother's day_, dear Grandma,
   Happy _Halloween_ to you.

2. **A** Did you get any _Valentine_ cards?
   B Yes, I did. Listen to this.
   Roses are red. Violets are blue.
   *You are my _lover_*
   And I love you.
   A Wow! Do you know who it's from?
   B No idea!

3. **A** Wake up, Mommy!
   Happy _Mother's day_!
   B Thank you. Oh, what beautiful flowers, and a cup of coffee!
   A And I made you a card! Look!
   B It's beautiful. What a sweet boy!

4. **A** Congratulations!
   B Thank you very much!
   A When's the big day?
   B Excuse me?
   A When's your _wedding_ day?
   B June 26. Didn't you get your invitation?

5. **A** It's midnight! Happy _New Year_ everybody!
   B Happy _New Year_!
   C Happy _New Year_!

6. **A** Thank goodness! It's Friday!
   B Yeah. Have a nice _Friday_!
   A Same to you.

7. **A** Ugh! Work again. I hate Monday mornings!
   B Me, too. Did you have a good _weekend_?
   A Yes, I did. It was great.

CD2 42 Listen and check.

Music of English 🎵

Work with a partner. Choose a conversation from Exercise 3. Learn it by heart. Pay attention to stress and intonation. Act it out for the class.

---

9 Food you like!

● **Grammar:** Count and noncount
nouns • *I like/I'd like* • *Some/
any* • *Much/many*
● **Vocabulary:** Food
Everyday English: Polite requests

STARTER What's your favorite • fruit? • vegetable? • drink?

Write your answers. Compare them with a partner, then with the class.

FOOD AND DRINK
Count and noncount nouns

1 Match the food and drink with the photos.
Which list has plural nouns, **A** or **B**?

A				B			
p ✓	apple juice	✓	pizza	✓	apples	✓	peas
	tea	✓	pasta		oranges	✓	tomatoes
	coffee	✓	cheese		bananas		hamburgers
	milk	✓	fish		strawberries		French fries
	soda	✓	chocolate		carrots	✓	cookies

2 **CD3 2** Listen to Daisy and Tom talking about what they
like and don't like. Put a check (✓) next to the food and
drink that Daisy likes. What doesn't Tom like?

3 Who says these things? Write **D** or **T**.

_____ **I don't like** coffee **at all**.

_____ **I like** orange juice, but I **don't like** oranges.

_____ **I don't like** fruit **very much at all**.

_____ **I really like** bananas.

_____ **I like** all fruit.

_____ **I like** vegetables, **especially** carrots and peas.

4 Talk about the lists of food and drink with a partner. What do
you like? What do you really like? What don't you like?

> ### GRAMMAR SPOT
>
> 1 Look at the pairs of sentences. What is the difference?
>
> | Chocolate **is** delicious. | Strawberries **are** delicious. |
> | Apple juice **is** good for you. | Apples **are** good for you. |
>
> 2 Can we count apple juice? Can we count apples?
>
> ▶▶ **Grammar Reference 9.1 p. 119**

I like . . . and I'd like . . .

1 `CD3 3` Read and listen to the conversation between Tom and Daisy's mom.

> **M** Hello, Tom. Would you like some milk or water?
>
> **T** I'd like some juice, if that's OK.
>
> **M** Of course. Would you like some orange juice?
>
> **T** Yes, please. I'd love some.
>
> **M** And would you like a chocolate chip cookie?
>
> **T** Oh, yes, please! Thank you very much.
>
> **M** You're welcome.

2 Practice the conversation in Exercise 1 with a partner. Then have similar conversations about other food and drink.

> Would you like some tea?

> No, thanks. I don't like tea very much.

GRAMMAR SPOT

1 Look at the sentences. What is the difference?

| Do you like tea? | Would you like some tea? |
| I like cookies. | I'd like a cookie. (I'd = I would) |

Which sentences mean *Do you want/I want . . .* ?

2 Look at these sentences.

> I'd like some bananas. (plural noun)
> I'd like some mineral water. (noncount noun)

We use *some* with both plural and noncount nouns.

3 Look at these questions.

> Would you like some peas?   Are there any peas?
>   **but**
> Can I have some coffee?   Is there any coffee?

We use *some*, not *any*, when we request and offer things.
We use *any*, not *some*, in other questions and negatives.

▶▶ **Grammar Reference 9.2 and 9.3 p. 119**

PRACTICE

Questions and answers

1 Choose *Would/Do you like . . . ?* or *I/I'd like . . .* .

1. *Would/Do* you like a tuna salad sandwich?
   No, thanks. I'm not hungry.
2. *Do/Would* you like Ella?
   Yes. She's very nice.
3. *Do/Would* you like a cold drink?
   Yes, soda, please.
4. Can I help you?
   Yes. *I/I'd like* some stamps, please.
5. What sports do you do?
   Well, *I/I'd like* swimming very much.
6. Excuse me, are you ready to order?
   Yes. *I/I'd like* a steak, please.

`CD3 4` Listen and check. Practice with a partner.

2 `CD3 5` Listen and choose the correct answers.

1. ☐ I like all sorts of fruit.
   ☑ Yes. I'd like some fruit, please.
2. ☑ I'd like a book by John Grisham.
   ☑ I like books by John Grisham.
3. ☑ I'd like a new bike.
   ☐ I like riding my bike.
4. ☐ I'd like a cat but not a dog.
   ☑ I like cats, but I don't like dogs.
5. ☑ I like Italian food, especially pasta.
   ☑ I'd like a plate of pasta.
6. ☑ No, thanks. I don't like ice cream.
   ☑ I'd like some ice cream, please.

`CD3 6` Listen and check. Practice with a partner.

a or some?

3 Write *a*, *an*, or *some*.

1. __a__ strawberry
2. __some__ fruit
3. __a__ banana
4. __some__ bread
5. __some__ milk
6. __some__ meat
7. __a__ apple
8. __a__ toast
9. __some__ money
10. __a__ dollar
11. __a__ notebook
12. __some__ homework

4 Write *a*, *an*, or *some*.

1. __a__ egg   2. __some__ eggs

3. __a__ cookie   4. __some__ cookies

5. __a__ (cup of) coffee   6. __some__ coffee

7. __a__ ice cream cone   8. __some__ ice cream

AT THE MARKET
some/any, much/many

1 What can you see at the market? Talk about the photo. Use *some/any* and *not much/not* many.

> There's some cheese.
> There aren't many cakes.
> There isn't much bread.
> There aren't any potatoes.

GRAMMAR SPOT

1 We use *many* with count nouns in questions and negatives.
How many cakes are there?   There **aren't many** cakes.

2 We use *much* with noncount nouns in questions and negatives.
How much bread is there?   There **isn't much** bread.

▶▶ **Grammar Reference 9.4 p. 119**

2 Read the shopping list. Ask and answer questions about what there is in the market.

Things to buy

- ☐ bread
- ☐ eggs
- ☐ milk
- ☐ butter
- ☐ apples
- ☐ cookies
- ☐ potatoes
- ☐ carrots
- ☐ strawberries
- ☐ tomatoes
- ☐ apple juice
- ☐ cake
- ☐ cheddar cheese
- ☐ tea

> Is there any bread?
> Yes, there is some.
> How much is there?
> There isn't much.
>
> Is there any milk?
> No, there isn't.
>
> Are there any apples?
> Yes, there are.
> How many are there.
> A lot.

3 **CD3** **7** Tom and his mom are at the market. Listen and put a check (✓) next to the things they buy from the list above. What don't they buy?

4 Look at the audio script on page 110. Work in groups of three. Practice the conversation.

PRACTICE

much or *many*?

1 Complete the questions using *much* or *many*.

1. How ~~many~~ people are there in the room?
2. How ~~much~~ gas is there in the car?
3. How ~~much~~ money do you have in your pocket?
4. How ~~many~~ eggs do we have?
5. How ~~much~~ milk is there in the refrigerator?
6. How ~~many~~ apples do you want?

2 Choose an answer for each question in Exercise 1.

   a. A kilo, please.
   b. There are two cartons.
   c. There are only two left.
   d. Only five dollars.
   e. Twenty. Nine men and eleven women.
   f. The tank is full.

3 Practice the questions and answers with a partner.

Check it

4 Correct the sentences.

1. How ~~much~~ potatoes do you want?
   How many potatoes do you want?
2. I don't like an ice cream.
3. Can I have a bread, please?
4. I'm hungry. I like a sandwich.
5. There isn't many milk left.
6. I'd like some fruits, please.
7. How many money do you have?
8. We have lot of homework today.

Role play

5 Work with a partner. Make a shopping list each. Buy the things you need in the market. Take turns to be the seller.

Can I help you?

   Yes, please. I'd like a/some . . .

Here you are. Anything else?

   Yes. Can I have a/some . . . ?

How much is that?

   That's . . . , please.

READING AND SPEAKING
Food around the world

1 Which food and drink comes from your country? Which foreign food and drink is popular in your country?

2 Can you identify any places or nationalities in the photos? What food can you see?

3 Read the text. Write the correct question heading for each paragraph.

> **Where does our food come from?**
>
> **What do we eat?**
>
> **How do we eat?**

Find lines in the text that match the photos.

4 Answer the questions.

1. When did human history start? Was it about 10,000 years ago or was it about 1 million years ago?
2. Do they eat much rice in the north of China?
3. Why do the Japanese eat a lot of fish?
4. Where don't people eat much fish?
5. Why do people in the middle of the U.S. eat more chicken and red meat?
6. How many courses are there in China?
7. How do people eat in the Middle East?
8. Why can we now eat most things at any time of the year?

What do you think?

5 Work in small groups and discuss these questions about your country.

1. What is a typical breakfast?
2. What does your family have for breakfast?
3. Is lunch or dinner the main meal of the day?
4. What is a typical main meal?

Writing

6 Write a paragraph about meals in your country. Use your ideas from Exercise 5.

Food
around the world

For **99%** of human history, people took their food from the world around them. They ate all that they could find, and then moved on. Then about 10,000 years ago, or for **1%** of human history, people learned to farm the land and control their environment.

The kind of food we eat depends on which part of the world we live in, or which part of our country we live in. For example, in the south of China they eat rice, but in the north they eat noodles. In Japan, people eat a lot of fish and other seafood. But in the middle of the United States, away from the sea, people don't eat so much fish, they eat more red meat and chicken. In Central Europe, people eat hundreds of different kinds of sausages.

In North America, Australia, and Europe there are two or more courses to every meal, and people eat with knives and forks. In China, all the food is together on the table, and they eat with chopsticks. In parts of India and the Middle East, people use their fingers and bread to pick up the food.

Nowadays it is possible to transport food easily from one part of the world to the other. We can eat what we like, when we like, at any time of the year. Bananas come from Central America or Africa; rice comes from California or Thailand; strawberries come from Chile or Mexico. Food is very big business. But people in poor countries are still hungry, and people in rich countries eat too much.

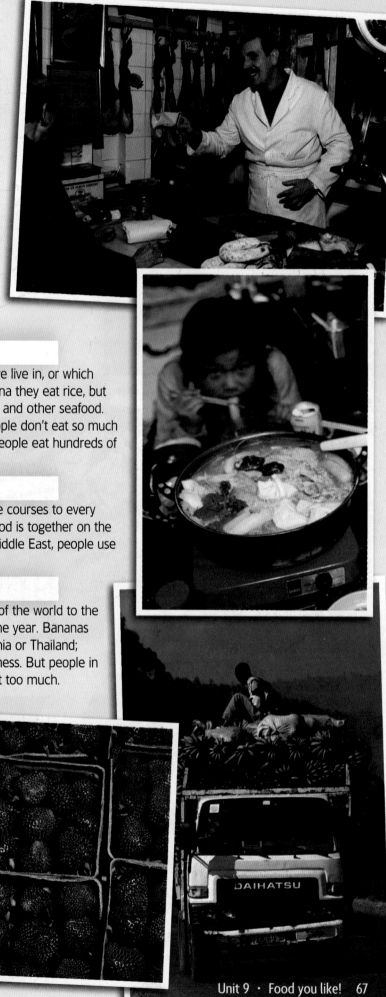

LISTENING AND SPEAKING
My favorite national food

1 Look at the photos of four national dishes. Which do you like? Match them with the countries.

| Italy | Argentina | the U.S. | Thailand |

2 Find these things in the photos.

| toast | tomatoes | chili peppers | onions | egg | bacon | pancakes | beef | noodles |

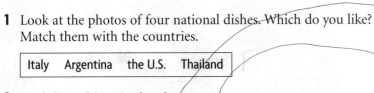

Bruschetta

Bife de chorizo

Pad Thai

American breakfast

3 **CD3** **8** Listen to the people. What nationality are they? Match them with their favorite food. What do they say about them?

Natalie

Danupol

Sergio

Giulia

4 Answer these questions about the people.

1. Who . . . ?
   - travels a lot
   - goes to cafes to eat their favorite food
   - likes noodles
   - eats their favorite food at home
2. How do you make pad thai?
3. Where is the best place to eat pad thai?
4. When does Natalie eat a big breakfast?
5. How do you make bruschetta?
6. Where is Giulia's favorite place to go?
7. How often does Sergio eat beef?
8. Who cooks it for him?

What do you think?

- What are *your* favorite national foods? When and where do you eat them?
- Describe them to your partner.

EVERYDAY ENGLISH
Polite requests

1 What can you see in the photograph?

2 Match the questions and responses.

1. Would you like some more carrots?
2. Could you pass the salt, please?
3. Could I have a glass of water, please?
4. Does anybody want more bread?
5. How would you like your coffee?
6. This is delicious! Can you give me the recipe?
7. Do you want help with the dishes?

Black, no sugar, please.
Yes, of course. I'm glad you like it.
Do you want bottled water or tap water?
Yes, please. They're delicious.
Yes, of course. Here you are.
Yes, please. I'd love some.
No, of course not. We have a dishwasher.

! We use *Can/Could I . . . ?* to ask for things.
Can I have a glass of water?
Could I have a glass of water?

We use *Can/Could you . . . ?* to ask other people to do things for us.
Can you give me the recipe?
Could you pass the salt?

CD3 9 Listen and check.

Music of English

CD3 10 Listen. Notice how the voice goes up at the end of a request. Practice the intonation.

Could you pass the salt, please?

Could I have a glass of water, please?

Can you give me the recipe?

Can I see the menu, please?

3 Complete these requests with *Can/Could I . . . ?* or *Can/Could you . . . ?*

1. _____ Can _____ have a cheese sandwich, please?
2. _____ Could _____ tell me the time, please?
3. _____ Could _____ take me to the station, please?
4. _____ Can _____ see the menu, please?
5. _____ Could _____ lend me some money, please?
6. _____ Could _____ help me with my homework, please?
7. _____ Could _____ borrow your dictionary, please?

4 Practice the requests with a partner. Give an answer for each request.

Can I have a cheese sandwich, please?

Yes, of course. That's $1.75.

CD3 11 Listen and compare your answers.

▶▶ **WRITING** Filling out forms *p. 100*   Unit 9 · Food you like!   69

10 Looking good!

- **Grammar:** Present continuous • *Whose?*
- **Vocabulary:** Clothes • Describing feelings
- **Everyday English:** In a clothing store

STARTER **1** Look around the classroom. Can you see any of these clothes?

a hat   a coat   a sweater   a shirt   a T-shirt   a dress   a skirt   a jacket
a suit   shorts   pants   jeans   shoes   boots   sneakers

2 What are you wearing?
What is your teacher wearing?
Tell the class.

> I'm wearing blue jeans and a white T-shirt.

> You're wearing a dress.

DESCRIBING PEOPLE
Present Continuous

1 Look at the photos. Describe the people.

Who ... ?
- is pretty
- is good-looking
- is handsome
  - is tall
  - isn't very tall

> Poppy's pretty.

Who has ... ?

long		
short	hair	
blonde		
dark	blue	eyes
gray	brown	

> Sofia has dark hair and brown eyes.

2 What are they doing?

Who ... ?
- is smiling
- is laughing
- is eating
- is standing up
- is drawing
- is reading
  - is sitting down
  - is using a computer
  - is painting
  - is walking

> Ella's smiling.

3 What are they wearing?

> Andy's wearing glasses.

> Simon's wearing a black jacket.

Andy

Alison, Ella, and Alfie

Poppy

1 *Am/is/are* + adjective describes people and things.

  She **is** young/tall/pretty.

2 *Am/is/are* + verb + *-ing* describes activities happening *now*. Complete the chart.

I		
You		learning English.
He/She		sitting in a classroom.
We	)	listening to the teacher.
They		

This is the Present Continuous tense.
What are the questions and the negatives?

3 What is the difference between these sentences?

  He speaks Spanish.
  He's speaking Spanish.

▶▶ **Grammar Reference 10.1 and 10.2 p. 120**

PRACTICE

Talking about you

1 Write sentences that are true for you at the moment.

1. I/wearing a jacket   *I'm not wearing a jacket, I'm wearing a sweater.*
2. I/wearing jeans
3. I/standing up
4. I/looking out of the window
5. It/raining

6. teacher/writing
7. We/working hard
8. I/chewing gum

Tell a partner about yourself.

2 Work with a partner.
Student A Choose someone in the classroom, but don't say who.
Student B Ask Yes/No questions to find out who it is!

Is it a woman?
Yes, it is.
Is she sitting near the window?
No, she isn't.
Does she have blonde hair?
No, she doesn't.

3 Look out the window. What can you see? Buildings? Hills? Fields? Can you see any people? What are they doing? Describe the scene.

Simon

Naomi

Colin

Kate and Sofia

Jake and Peter

Who's at the wedding?

4 **CD3** **12** Alan is at Mike's wedding, but he doesn't know anyone. Mike is telling him about the other guests. Listen and write the people's names on the picture.

Bill John George James Fiona Sue *(handwritten on picture)*

5 Listen again and complete the chart.

	Present Continuous	Present Simple
George	He's sitting down and he's talking to James.	He works in LA.
James	*He is talking to George*	*He teaches math*
Fiona	*She drinking coffee*	*She is a writer*
Sue	*Wearing red suit*	*She is a nurse*
Bill and John	*their eating cake are*	*their lives is sister*

Getting information

6 Work with a partner.

Student A Look at the picture of a party on page 124.
Student B Look at the picture of a party on page 126.

Don't show your picture! There are *ten* differences. Talk about the pictures to find them.

> In my picture three people are dancing.

> In my picture four people are dancing.

> There's a woman with brown hair.

> Is she wearing a black dress?

A DAY IN THE PARK
Whose is it?

1 Find these things in the picture.

a baseball cap   a bicycle   a dog   flowers   sneakers a coat   sunglasses   an umbrella   headphones a soccer ball   a skateboard

2 **CD3** **13** Listen to the questions. Complete the answers with *his*, *hers*, or *theirs*.

1. Whose baseball cap is this?   It's *his*.
2. Whose flowers are these?   They're *hers*.
3. Whose dog is this?   It's *theirs*.

Practice the questions and answers with a partner. Then ask about the other things in Exercise 1.

3 Give something of yours to the teacher. Ask and answer questions about the objects. Use these possessive pronouns.

mine   yours   his   hers   ours   theirs

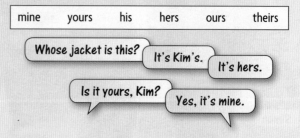

> Whose jacket is this?   It's Kim's.   It's hers.

> Is it yours, Kim?   Yes, it's mine.

PRACTICE

who's or whose?

1 Choose the correct word. Compare your answers with a partner.

1. I like *your* / *yours* house.
2. *Ours* / *Our* house is smaller than *their* / *theirs*.
3. And *their* / *theirs* backyard is bigger than *our* / *ours*, too.
4. *My* / *Mine* children are older than *her* / *hers*.
5. *Whose* / *Who's* talking to *your* / *yours* sister?
6. This book isn't *my* / *mine*. Is it *your* / *yours*?
7. "*Whose* / *Who's* dictionary is this?" "It's *his* / *him*."
8. "*Whose* / *Who's* going to the party tonight?" "I'm not."
9. "*Whose* / *Who's* dog is running around *our* / *ours* backyard?"

2 **CD3 14** Listen to the sentences. If the word is **Whose?** shout 1! If the word is **Who's?** shout 2!

Who's on the phone? 　　**Whose** is it?

What a mess!

3 **CD3 15** The house is a mess! Complete the conversation. Listen and check.

A _Whose_ tennis racket _is_ this?

B It's _mine_.

A What's it doing here?

B I'm _playing_ tennis this afternoon.

> The Present Continuous can also describe activities happening in the near future.
>
> **I'm playing** tennis this afternoon.
> **We're having** pizza for dinner tonight.

4 Make more conversations with a partner.

1. sunglasses *is* these? / John's / going to the beach later
2. shoes *is* these? / Mary's / going dancing tonight
3. suitcase *is* this? / mine / going on vacation tomorrow
4. coat *is* this? / Jane's / going for a walk soon
5. plane ticket *is* this? / Jo's / flying to Houston this afternoon
6. glasses *is* these? / ours / having a party tonight

CD3 16 Listen and check.

Check it

5 Correct the sentences.

1. Alice is tall and she has long, black hairs.
2. Who's boots are these?
3. I'm wearing a jeans.
4. Look at Roger. He stands next to Jeremy.
5. He's work in a bank. He's the manager.
6. What is drinking Suzie?
7. Whose that man in the backyard?
8. Where you going tonight?
9. What you do after school today?

GRAMMAR SPOT

1 Complete the chart.

Subject	Object	Adjective	Pronoun
I	me	my	mine
You	you	your	yours
He	him	his	his
She	her	her	hers
We	us	our	ours
They	them	their	theirs

2 *Whose . . . ?* asks about possession.

Whose hat is this?　|　It's mine. = It's my hat.
Whose is it?

3 Careful!

Who's your teacher?　　Who's = Who is

▶▶ **Grammar Reference 10.3 p. 120**

LISTENING AND SPEAKING
Looking for that something

1 What makes you happy? Think of five things that make you happy. Write them down. Compare them with a partner.

2 What makes you happiest? Choose one thing only. Compare with the class.

3 **CD3 17** Close your books and listen to the song.

4 Read the song by an Irish band called Westlife.

Can you match these words from the song and their meanings?

joy	to love
to cherish	happiness
to deny	when the sun comes up
solitary	to say no to something
the sunrise	alone, lonely

5 **CD3 17** Look at the words on the right. Choose the correct word to complete the lines. Listen again and check.

What do you think?

- In the song, what does "flying without wings" mean?
- Did you find any of the things on your list in the song?

Everybody's _____ for that something   **looking / finding**
One thing that makes it all complete
You find it in the strangest _____   **places / houses**
Places you never knew it could be

Some find it in the faces of their _____   **parents / children**
Some find it in their lover's _____   **hair / eyes**
Who can deny the joy it brings
When you find that _____ thing   **special / interesting**
You're flying without wings

Some find it sharing every _____   **breakfast / morning**
Some in their solitary lives
You find it in the words of others
A simple line can make you _____ or cry   **dance / laugh**

You find it in the deepest _____   **friendship / water**
The kind you cherish all your life
And when you know how _____ that means   **many / much**
You've found that special thing
You're flying without wings

So impossible as it may seem
You've got to _____ for every dream   **fight / sleep**
'Cause who's to _____ which one you let go   **say / know**
Would have made you complete

Well, for me it's waking up beside _____   **her / you**
To watch the sunrise on your face
To know that I can say I _____ you   **like / love**
At any given time or place

It's little things that only I know
Those are the things that make you _____   **mine / theirs**
And it's like flying without wings
'Cause you're my special _____   **person / thing**
I'm flying without wings

You're the place my life _____   **begins / stops**
And you'll be where it ends
I'm flying without wings
And that's the joy you _____   **take / bring**
I'm flying without wings

Flying
without wings

6 Read the questionnaire and answer the questions. Stand up. Ask students in the class the questions. Find people with the same answers as yours.

My favorite things

1. What's your favorite food?
   _____

2. What's your favorite drink?
   _____

3. What's your favorite color?
   _____

4. What are your favorite clothes?
   _____

5. What are your favorite shoes?
   _____

6. Who's your favorite singer or band?
   _____

7. What are your favorite things to do on weekends?
   _____

8. Who's your favorite person?
   _____

9. Where's your favorite place?
   _____

10. Who's your favorite movie star or actor?
    _____

7 Tell the class which people like the same things as you.

> Johann and I both like blue.
>> Stella and I both like sneakers.

▶▶ **WRITING** Describing people *p. 101*

VOCABULARY
Describing feelings

1 Match the feelings to the pictures.

bored tired worried excited annoyed interested

2 Match the feelings and reasons to make sentences.

	Feelings		Reasons
I am	bored tired worried excited annoyed interested	because	I'm going on vacation tomorrow. we have a good teacher. I worked very hard today. I can't find my keys. I have nothing to do. I want to go to the party but I can't.

> **!** Some adjectives can end in both *-ed* and *-ing*.
> I was **interested** in the book.
> The book was **interesting**.
> The students were **bored**.
> The lesson was **boring**.

3 Complete each sentence with the correct adjective.

1. excited / exciting
   - Life in New York is very …
   - The football fans were very …

2. tired / tiring
   - The marathon runners were very …
   - That game of tennis was very …

3. annoyed / annoying
   - The child's behavior was really …
   - The teacher was … when nobody did the homework.

4. worried / worrying
   - The news is very …
   - Everybody was very … when they heard the news.

4 Answer your teacher's questions using adjectives from Exercises 1 and 2.

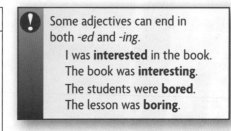

Did you like doing Exercise 2?

No, we didn't. It was very boring!

How did you feel?

Very bored!

EVERYDAY ENGLISH
In a clothing store

1 Read the lines of a conversation in a clothing store. Who says them, the customer or the salesperson? Write **C** or **SP**.

a. **SP** Can I help you?

b. **C** Oh, yes. I like that one much better. Can I try it on?

c. **SP** $39.99. How do you want to pay?

d. **C** Yes, please. I'm looking for a shirt to go with my new jeans.

e. **C** Blue.

f. **SP** Yes, of course. The fitting rooms are over there.

   ... Is the size OK?

g. **C** OK. I'll take the green. How much is it?

h. **C** Can I pay by credit card?

i. **SP** What color are you looking for?

j. **C** No, it isn't the right blue.

k. **C** No, it's a bit too big. Do you have a smaller size?

l. **SP** That's the last blue one we have, I'm afraid. But we have it in green.

m. **SP** Well, what about this one? It's a bit darker blue.

n. **SP** What about this one? Do you like this?

o. **SP** Credit card's fine. Thank you very much.

2 Can you match any lines with the photos?

Photo 1 **SP** *Can I help you?*
             C *Yes, please. I'm looking for a shirt to go with my new jeans.*

3 Work with a partner and put the lines in the correct order.

CD3 18 Listen and check.

> **Music *of* English** ♫♪
>
> Practice the conversation with your partner. Pay attention to stress and intonation.

4 Make more conversations in a clothing store. Buy some different clothes.

11 Life's an adventure!

STARTER

1 How many sentences can you make?

2 Make similar true sentences about you. Tell the class.

I'm going to Brazil	soon.
I went to Brazil	when I was a student.
	next month.
	in a year.
	two years ago.
	when I retire.

FUTURE PLANS
going to

1 Jack and his coach, Danny Carrick, both have plans for the future. Read their future plans. Which do you think are Jack's? Which are Danny's? Write **J** or **D**.

1. ___J___ I'm going to be a soccer player.
2. ___D___ I'm going to travel all over the world.
3. ___D___ I'm going to train very hard.
4. ___D___ I'm going to try new things.
5. ___J___ I'm going to play for a Major League Soccer team.
6. ___D___ I'm not going to marry until I'm very old.
7. ___D___ I'm not going to stay at home and watch TV.
8. ___D___ I'm going to learn to scuba dive.
9. ___D___ I'm going to write a book.
10. ___J___ I'm going to be famous.

CD3 19 Listen and check. Were you correct?

2 Talk first about Jack, then about Danny. Use the ideas in Exercise 1.

> Jack's going to be a soccer player.

> He's going to ...

> He isn't going to ...

Which two plans are the same for both of them?

> They're both going to ...

3 **CD3 20** Listen and repeat the questions and answers about Jack.

> Is he going to be a soccer player?

> Yes, he is.

> What's he going to do?

> Train very hard.

When I grow up...

Jack, age 11

When I retire

Danny Carrick, age 58

GRAMMAR SPOT

1 The verb *to be* + *going to* expresses future plans. Complete the chart.

I	am	
You	are	
He/She	is	going to leave tomorrow.
We	are	
They	are	

What are the questions and the negatives?

2 Is there much difference between these two sentences?

    I'm leaving tomorrow.   I'm going to leave tomorrow.

▶▶ **Grammar Reference 11.1 p. 121**

PRACTICE

Questions about Jack

1 With a partner, make more questions about Jack. Then match them with an answer.

Questions
1. Why/he/train very hard?
2. How long/play soccer?
3. When/marry?
4. How many children/have?
5. Who/teach to play?

Answers
a. Until he's 35.
b. Two.
c. His sons.
d. Not until he's very old—about 25!
e. Because he wants to be a soccer player.

2 **CD3 21** Listen and check. Practice the questions and answers with your partner.

Questions about you

3 Are you going to do any of these things after class? Ask and answer the questions with a partner.

1. watch TV
2. have coffee
3. catch a bus
4. eat in a restaurant
5. meet some friends
6. cook a meal
7. go shopping
8. wash your hair
9. do your homework

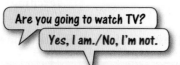

Are you going to watch TV?
Yes, I am./No, I'm not.

4 Tell the class some of the things you and your partner *are* or *are not* going to do.

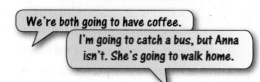

We're both going to have coffee.
I'm going to catch a bus, but Anna isn't. She's going to walk home.

EXCITING VACATIONS

Comparative adjectives

1 What is your perfect vacation? Which do you prefer?

- a beach vacation
- a ski trip
- a hiking vacation in the mountains
- a sightseeing vacation in a city

2 Match an adjective with its opposite. Which adjectives do you think best describe the vacations in Exercise1?

cheap relaxing boring safe	stressful dangerous exciting expensive

3 **CD3 22** Listen to Tony and Amanda talking about their next vacation. Which vacation do you think they will choose? Why?

Much more than...

4 Write the correct form of the adjectives.

1. **A** I think a vacation in Los Angeles is __cheaper__ (cheap) than a vacation in Miami.

   B I don't think so. Los Angeles is much __more__ __expensive__ (expensive)

2. **A** I think Boston is _____ (small) and _____ (old) than New York.

   B Well, you're right, Boston *is* _____ (small), but it's *not* _____ (old).

3. **A** A ski trip is going to be _____ _____ (exciting) than hiking in the mountains.

   B I don't agree. Hiking is much _____ _____ (exciting).

4. **A** I think mountain climbing is much _____ _____ (dangerous) than sky diving.

   B Really? I think they're both very frightening. I don't think one is _____ (safe) than the other.

5. **A** Which city do you think is _____ (good), Mexico City or Buenos Aires?

   B I don't know. I think they're both great. I don't think one is _____ _____ (exciting) than the other.

CD3 23 Listen and check. Practice the conversations with a partner.

GRAMMAR SPOT

1 Complete these comparatives. What are the rules?

I'm _____ (old) than you.
Your class is _____ (noisy) than my class.
Your car was _____ (expensive) than my car.

2 What are the comparatives of the adjectives in the boxes?

3 The comparatives of *good* and *bad* are irregular. What are they?

good _____   bad _____

▶▶ **Grammar Reference 11.2 p. 121**

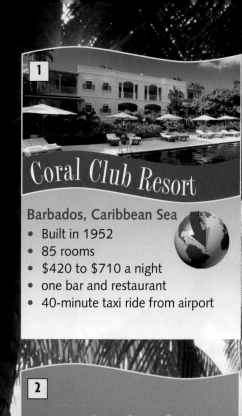

Coral Club Resort

Barbados, Caribbean Sea

- Built in 1952
- 85 rooms
- $420 to $710 a night
- one bar and restaurant
- 40-minute taxi ride from airport

Palm Hotel Resort

Maldives, Indian Ocean

- Built in 1998
- 98 rooms
- $200 to $600 a night
- two bars and two restaurants
- 50-minute boat ride from airport

Bati Island Resort

Fiji, Pacific Ocean

- Built in 1992
- 7 rooms
- $660 to $770 a night
- one bar and restaurant
- one hour seaplane flight from airport

PARADISE ISLANDS
Superlative adjectives

1 Look at the pictures of some of the world's most relaxing vacation resorts on page 80. Which one do you like best?

2 Read the information about them. Are the sentences true (✓) or false (✗)? Correct the false sentences. What is the same about the true (✓) sentences?

1. The Coral Club is cheaper than the Palm Hotel.
2. Bati Island is the most expensive resort.
3. The Coral Club is newer than the Palm Hotel.
4. The Palm Hotel is the newest resort.
5. The Coral Club is bigger than the Palm Hotel.
6. The Palm Hotel is the biggest resort.
7. Bati Island is the smallest resort.
8. Bati Island is nearer to the airport than the Palm Hotel.
9. The Coral Club is the nearest to the airport.
10. Bati Island is the farthest from the airport.

GRAMMAR SPOT

1 Complete these superlative sentences. What's the rule?

The Palm Hotel is the _____ (cheap).

Bati Island is the _____ _____ (expensive).

2 Dictionaries often show irregular comparative and superlative forms of adjectives. Look at this:

good /gʊd/ *adj.* (**better**, **best**)

Complete these irregular forms:

bad /bæd/ *adj.* (_____, _____)

far /fɑr/ *adj.* (_____, _____)

▶▶ **Grammar Reference 11.2 p. 121**

PRACTICE

The biggest and best!

1 Complete the conversations using the superlative form of the adjective.

1. Mount Everest is a very big mountain.

   Yes, _it's the biggest mountain_____ in the world.

2. The Lakers are a very famous basketball team.

   Yes, I think _____ in the world.

3. The Ritz is a very expensive hotel.

   Yes, _____ in the city.

4. New York's a very cosmopolitan city.

   Yes, _____ in the world.

5. Brad Pitt is a very popular movie star.

   Yes, _____ in America.

6. Miss Smith is a very funny teacher.

   Yes, _____ in our school.

7. Anna is a very intelligent student.

   Yes, _____ in the class.

8. This is a very easy exercise.

   Yes, _____ in the book.

CD3 24 Listen and check. What other information do you hear?

Talking about your class

2 How well do you know the other students in your class? Describe them using these adjectives and others.

| tall   small   old   young   intelligent   funny |

> I think Ivan is the tallest in the class. He's taller than Karl.

> Sofia's the youngest.

> I'm the most intelligent!

Check it

3 Correct the sentences.

1. I'm the most young in the class.
2. She's taller and most intelligent that her brother.
3. Last week I was much busyer than this week.
4. My homework is the worse in the class. Yours is the most good.
5. Yesterday was more warm than today.
6. Is going to rain and be more cold tomorrow.
7. Are you going wash your hair this evening?
8. This exercise is most difficult in the book.

READING AND SPEAKING
Born free

1 Which of these sports do you think is the most dangerous? Put them in order 1–6. 1 is the *most* dangerous. Compare your ideas with a partner and then the class.

_____ skiing   _____ soccer   _____ mountain climbing
_____ windsurfing   _____ golf   _____ scuba diving

2 Match a verb with a noun or phrase.

jump	a medal
take	over a wall
win	underwater
swim	a record
break	oxygen
breathe	a class

3 Look at the photos of Tanya Streeter and David Belle. Do you know what the sport is? Work in two groups.

Group A Read about Tanya.
Group B Read about David.

Answer the questions about your person.
Check your answers with your group.

1. Where did she/he grow up? *Cayman France*
2. What did she/he like doing as a child? *run climb jump*
3. How did she/he become interested in the sport? *peace quiet*
4. How does she/he feel when he/she does the sport? *freedom*
5. How dangerous is the sport? *No oxygean*
6. Does she/he teach the sport? *Yes*
7. What did she/he do last year? *television first time*
8. What are her/his future plans? *teach diving*

4 Work with a partner from the other group. Compare Tanya and David, using your answers.

Speaking

5 **Group A** Make questions to ask David.

1. Why/like the countryside?
2. What/like doing at school?
3. What sport/invent?
4. What/do in Lisses?
5. What/do next?

Group B Make questions to ask Tanya.

1. What/like doing as a child?
2. When/take a diving class?
3. How long/can/swim underwater?
4. What record/break?
5. What/do next?

6 Work with a partner from the other group. Interview each other.

Free diving

As a child, **Tanya Streeter** always loved swimming in the sea – she grew up in the Cayman Islands in the Caribbean. She could always dive the deepest for seashells. But she didn't know then that she could dive deeper than anyone else in the world.

Tanya discovered her diving abilities in 1997, when she took a class in free diving. Free diving is a new sport. It's very dangerous, because you dive with no oxygen. There were only men in the class and no one wanted to dive with her because she was a girl. But her class was surprised when they saw how long she could swim underwater. Her teachers immediately wanted to train her. A few months later, Tanya started breaking records. She can swim underwater for nearly six minutes with just one breath! Last year she broke the world free diving record. She dove 121 meters with one breath.

She says: "At the bottom of the sea I'm calm. I love the peace and quiet down there. Coming up again is very difficult. You can't think about the pain!

I'm not planning to break any more records for a while. I'm going to wait and see if anyone breaks my last record! In the future I'm going to teach free diving and work for sea-life conservation."

Free running

David Belle grew up in the countryside, and he always loved the feeling of freedom there. He liked running, jumping, and climbing trees in the woods when he was a child. At the age of nine, he and his family went to live in Lisses, a town outside Paris. But he continued to jump and climb there. He loved doing gymnastics at school.

As a teenager in 1989, David invented the sport of Le Parkour or "free running." The idea of Le Parkour is to find new and often dangerous ways to travel across the town. The runners or "traceurs" work in groups. They run and jump over walls, roofs, and buildings—everything! They try to move like cats. David and his friend Sebastian spent ten years in Lisses practicing their moves and jumps, and teaching other people. Last year they were on television for the first time. David says that Le Parkour is an art and a philosophy, not a sport. They are not trying to win medals. They just want to learn new moves and do them well. They like to feel free.

David says: "We do it because we need to move. We are going to take our art to the world and show people how to move. And we are going to go where no human ever went before."

VOCABULARY AND SPEAKING
The weather

1 Match the words and symbols.

sunny	rainy 4	windy	snowy 2	cloudy	foggy

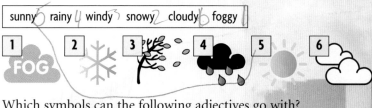

1	2	3	4	5	6
FOG					

Which symbols can the following adjectives go with?

hot	warm	cold	cool	wet	dry

2 **CD3** **25** Listen and complete the answers.

A What's the weather like today?
B It's _____ and it's very _____ .
A What was it like yesterday?
B Oh, it was _____ and _____ .
A What's it going to be like tomorrow?
B I think it's going to be _____ .

 The question *What . . . like?* asks for a description.
What's the weather like? = Tell me about the weather.

Practice the questions and answers. Ask and answer about the weather where *you* are.

3 Work with a partner. Find out about the weather around the world yesterday.

Student A Look at the information on this page.
Student B Go to page 126.

Ask and answer questions to complete the information.

WORLD WEATHER
NOON YESTERDAY

		°F
Atlanta	S	86
Boston		
Brasilia	S	75
Denver		
Hong Kong	R	60
London		
Los Angeles	Fg	70
Mexico City		
San Francisco	Fg	50
São Paulo		
Seattle	R	42
Toronto		
Vancouver	Sn	40

S = sunny
C = cloudy
Fg = foggy
R = rainy
Sn = snowy

What was the weather like in Atlanta?

It was sunny and hot. Eighty-six degrees.

4 Which city was the hottest? Which was the coldest? Which month do you think it is?

EVERYDAY ENGLISH
Making suggestions

1 Make a list of things you can do in good weather and things you can do in bad weather. Compare your list with a partner.

Good weather	Bad weather
Go to the beach	Watch TV

2 **CD3 26** Read and listen to the beginning of two conversations. Complete B's suggestions.

1 A It's a beautiful day! What should we do?
  B Let's _____!

2 A It's raining again! What should we do?
  B Let's _____ and _____ .

> **!** **1** We use *should* to ask for and make suggestions.
>   What should we do? = What do you want to do?
>   Should we go swimming? = I suggest that we go swimming.
>
>   **2** We use *Let's* to make a suggestion for everyone.
>   Let's go! = I suggest that we all go. (Let's = Let us)
>   Let's have a pizza!

3 Continue the two conversations in Exercise 2 with these lines. Put them in the correct order a–c.

		Well, let's go to the beach.
		OK. What movie do you want to see?
1	a	Oh no! It's too hot to play tennis.
		But we watched a DVD last night.
		I'll get my bathing suit.
		Well, let's go to the movies.

CD3 27 Listen and check. Practice the conversations with your partner. Pay attention to stress and intonation.

4 Have more conversations suggesting what to do when the weather is good or bad. Use your lists of activities in Exercise 1 to help you.

▶▶ **WRITING** Writing a postcard *p. 102*

85

12 Have you ever?

- **Grammar:** Present Perfect • *ever, never, yet,* and *just*
- **Vocabulary:** City and country words
- **Everyday English:** At the airport

STARTER **1** Match the countries and flags.

Thailand | Brazil 5 | France 4
Mexico 2 | Great Britain 7
Spain 3 | Japan 6 | Korea 9
Egypt | the U.S 8

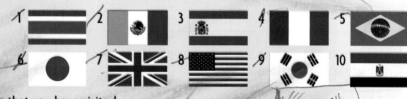

1 2 3 4 5
6 7 8 9 10

2 Put a check (✓) next to the countries that you have visited.

IN MY LIFE
Present Perfect + *ever* and *never*

1 **CD3 28** Listen to Steve and Ryan's conversation. What are they talking about? Who's Tara?

2 **CD3 29** Read and listen to Ryan's answers. Then listen and repeat.

> I've been to Paris. (I've = I have)
> I haven't been to Barcelona.
> I've been to Italy.
> I've never been to Venice.
> She's been to Mexico. (She's = She has)
> She hasn't been anywhere in Europe!

Work in groups. Look at the flags. Tell each other which countries you have or haven't visited. Have you been to any other countries?

3 **CD3 30** Read and listen to Tara and Steve's conversation. Practise with a partner.

T Have you ever been to Barcelona?
S No, I haven't.
T Have you ever been to Paris?
S Yes, I have.
T When did you go?
S Two years ago.
T Did you like it?
S Yes, it was beautiful.

MELBOURNE
AUSTRALIA

EL CAPITAN — SUNSET
YOSEMITE NATIONAL PARK, CALIFORNIA
Rising over 3,245 feet above the valley floor, El Capitan is one of the largest exposed monoliths in the world.
© Photograph by Chris Loberg

Hi guys!
San Francisco is fantastic! We are having a superb time - and are trying to see all the sights. We're staying near the Yosemite National Park, which is just beautiful.
See you guys soon (probably reading this with you actually)
Nicky

The weather is fantastic. We went to an Aussie football match yesterday and are off to a winery & then a 'barbie' tomorrow.

Stephanie Richards
14 Cobhill Gardens
Chipping Norton
Oxon
ENGLAND   POSTCODE

4 Write down the names of four cities in your country or another country that you have visited. Have similar conversations with your partner.

5 Tell the class about your partner.

> Maria's been to Seoul. (Maria's = Maria has)
>
> She went there two years ago.
>
> But she hasn't been to Tokyo./
> She's never been to Tokyo. (She's = She has)

TULUM

GRAMMAR SPOT

1 We use the Present Perfect to talk about experiences in our lives.
Have you ever (at any time in your life) been to Toronto?

2 We use the Past Simple to say exactly *when* something happened.
When did you go to Toronto?

| I went there | two years ago. |
| | in 2006. |

3 We make the Present Perfect tense with *has/have* + the past participle. Complete the chart.

	Affirmative	Negative	
I You We They	have have have have	haven't haven't haven't haven't	been to Toronto.
He She It	has has has	hasn't hasn't hasn't	

4 Write *ever* and *never* in the right place in these sentences.
Has he _ever_ been to Tokyo?
He's _never_ been to Tokyo.

▶▶ **Grammar Reference 12.1 p. 121**

PRACTICE

Past participles

1 Here are the past participles of some verbs. Write the infinitive.

eaten	_eat_	made	_make_	given	_give_
seen	_see_	taken	_take_	won	_win_
met	_meet_	ridden	_ride_	had	_have_
drunk	_drink_	cooked	_cook_	stayed	_stay_
flown	_flown_	bought	_buy_	done	_do_

2 Which are the two regular verbs?

3 What are the Past Simple forms of the verbs?

4 Look at the list of irregular verbs on page 133 and check your answers.

What has Ryan done?

1 **CD3** **31** Listen to Ryan talking about his life and put a check (✓) next to the things he has done.

- ☐ lived in a foreign country
- ☐ worked for a big company
- ☐ stayed in an expensive hotel
- ☐ flown in a jumbo jet
- ☐ cooked a meal for a lot of people
- ☐ met a famous person
- ☐ seen a play by Shakespeare
- ☐ ridden a motorcycle
- ☐ been to the hospital
- ☐ won a competition

2 Tell your teacher about Ryan and answer your teacher's questions.

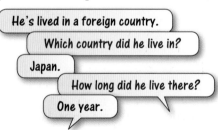

> He's lived in a foreign country.
> Which country did he live in?
> Japan.
> How long did he live there?
> One year.

3 Ask your teacher the questions from Exercise 1.

> Have you ever lived in a foreign country?
> Which country did you live in?

4 Ask a partner the questions. Tell the class about your partner.

A HONEYMOON IN VENICE
Present Perfect + *yet* and *just*

1 Ryan and Tara are on their honeymoon in Venice. Before they went, they made a list of things they wanted to do there. Read the list below.

> **VENICE**
>
> Things to do...
> - ☐ have coffee in St. Mark's Square
> - ☐ climb up the Bell Tower
> - ☐ see the paintings in the Doge's Palace
> - ☐ ride on a gondola
> - ☐ go on a boat ride along the Grand Canal
> - ☐ walk across the Rialto Bridge
> - ☐ visit the glass factories on Murano Island
> - ☐ go to the beach at the Lido

2 **CD3** **32** Tara is calling her sister Amy back home in the U.S. Listen to their conversation. Put a check (✓) next to the things in the list she and Ryan have done.

GRAMMAR SPOT

1 Complete the sentences.
   1. Have you _____ in a gondola yet?
   2. We _____ climbed up the Bell Tower yet.
   3. We just _____ on a boat ride along the Grand Canal.

2 Where do we put *yet* in a sentence? Where do we put *just* in a sentence?

3 We can only use *yet* with **two** of the following. Which two?
   - ☐ Affirmative sentences
   - ☐ Questions
   - ☐ Negative sentences

▶▶ **Grammar Reference 12.2 p. 122**

3 With a partner, talk about what Ryan and Tara have done and haven't done yet.

> They've had coffee in St. Mark's Square.
> They haven't climbed up the Bell Tower yet.

CD3 **32** Listen again and check.

Venice

PRACTICE

I just did it

1 Work with a partner. Make questions with *yet* and answers with *just*.

> **Have you called your mother yet?**
>
> **Yes, I just called her.**

1. do the dishes
2. have lunch
3. wash your hair
4. clean the car
5. make dinner
6. meet the new student
7. check your e-mail
8. give your homework to the teacher
9. finish the exercise

Check it

2 Put a check (✓) next to the correct sentence.

1. ☑ I saw Ryan yesterday.
   ☐ I've seen Ryan yesterday.
2. ☐ Did you ever eat Chinese food?
   ☑ Have you ever eaten Chinese food?
3. ☑ Tara won $5,000 last month.
   ☐ Tara has won $5,000 last month.
4. ☐ I've never drank Italian coffee.
   ☑ I've never drunk Italian coffee.
5. ☐ Steve has ever been to Taiwan.
   ☑ Steve has never been to Taiwan.
6. ☐ Has your sister yet had the baby?
   ☑ Has your sister had the baby yet?
7. ☑ I haven't done my homework yet.
   ☐ I've done my homework yet.
8. ☑ Did she just bought a new car?
   ☐ Did she just buy a new car?

READING AND SPEAKING
We've never learned to drive!

1 Work with a partner. Ask and answer the questions. Compare your answers with the class.

Have you ever ... ?	When? Where? Who with?
... walked a long way?	
... cycled a long way?	
... hitchhiked?	
... ridden a motorcycle?	
... ridden a camel	
... driven a tractor?	

2 Read the introduction to the article and look at the photos. What questions would you like to ask Josie and Russell?
Which countries have you been to?
Why ... never learned to drive?
... ever been frightened?
... ever had an accident?

3 Work in two groups.

Group A Read about Josie.
Group B Read about Russell.

Try to find the answers to your questions in Exercise 2.

4 Answer the questions.
1. What is her/his job? *teacher*
2. How did her/his love of travel start? *she told such... when she is... young*
3. When did she/he start traveling? *when she is young*
4. Where has she/he been? *to 43 countr...*
5. Does she/he travel alone or with other people? *alone*
6. What extreme weather conditions has she/he experienced? *travel*
7. What's the most frightening thing that has ever *driving* happened to her/him?
8. What does she/he like best about traveling? *she can*
9. What is she/he going to do next? *Europe see the distan...*

5 Find a partner from the other group. Compare your answers to the questions.

Language work

Find examples of the Present Perfect of these verbs in the article.

like	cycle	write	travel	learn	ride	make	visit

What do you think?

• Would you like to travel like Josie and Russell? Why/Why not?
• Do people cycle and hitchhike a lot in your country?
• What's your favorite way to travel? Why?

DRIVING?

Not for me, thanks. I'll walk, get the train, cycle, hitch ...

There are over 625 million cars in the world today, but some people just don't like them. Meet two great travelers who have been everywhere, but never behind a driving wheel.

Angela Matthews reports.

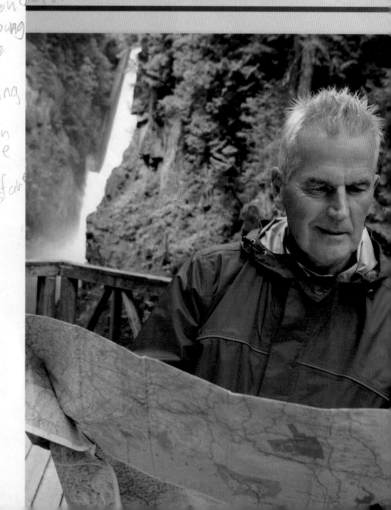

The woman at home on a bike

Josie Dew says it was her elementary school teacher who made her want to travel. "She told such wonderful stories about distant lands. I dreamed of visiting them one day." But after Josie fell out of a fast moving car when she was very young, she has never liked driving or being driven in anything with four wheels. She prefers two.

She has cycled all her life. She began touring when she was eleven, going around England and Scotland. Her first big tour was to Africa, cycling through Europe on her way to Tunisia and Algeria. She wrote a book about this trip, called *Wind in My Wheels*, and she has since written six more books.

When she's not cycling, she works as a professional chef. She says: "I work as hard as I can to pay for my next trip." She reckons she has cycled more than 300,000 miles in all five continents. She has been to over 43 countries. She has cycled through floods in the Himalayas, through baking deserts in Morocco, and through tornados in the U.S. She has often been near war zones, but has only had one really frightening experience. "A man attacked me while I was in Eastern Europe, and I had to escape."

She has sometimes cycled with friends, but she has mainly traveled alone. "What I like best is the sense of freedom. I meet more people when I'm on my own. People are so kind. They help me out and talk to me and I get to know people everywhere."

She has a daughter, Molly, who she takes with her on her cycling tours. "Molly has already been to Europe. Now we're planning a trip to Canada."

Life on the open road

When Russell Hartford was a child, he loved looking at maps. "I just think they are so exciting. I always knew that one day I would travel the world," he says. He was a teenager in the 1960s, and started hitchhiking because "everyone did it and it was free." His first trip was to Mexico when he was 17, and it was an adventure that opened his eyes.

He has never learned to drive because, he says: "I am hopeless with anything mechanical. I tried to drive once, but I backed into a wall, so I never tried again." When he got married, he and his new wife hitchhiked to Niagara Falls for their honeymoon.

He teaches geography at a college in Boston, so he usually waits for long school breaks to travel overseas. So far, he has been to over 40 countries in Europe, Latin America, Africa, and Asia. And he's gotten some strange rides. He's ridden on a motorcycle in Argentina, on a camel in Egypt, and on a tractor in China. Once he was standing on a highway in Alaska when it started to snow. "There was a snow storm and it was a complete whiteout. I couldn't see anything, and no one could see me. I nearly froze to death." The most danger he has ever been in was in Brazil, when a snake crossed the road right in front of him. "I later found out that it was a tropical rattlesnake—and very poisonous!"

He sometimes travels with his wife, but usually on his own. "The best thing for me is meeting people from different cultures." He has made a lot of friends, and some of them have visited him. He's now planning a trip around the coast of Australia, the only continent he's never seen.

VOCABULARY AND PRONUNCIATION
City and country words

1 Match these words with the pictures. Which things do you usually find only in the country?

woods park museum church farm bridge
parking lot port factory cafe field theater lake
village hill mountain cottage building river airport

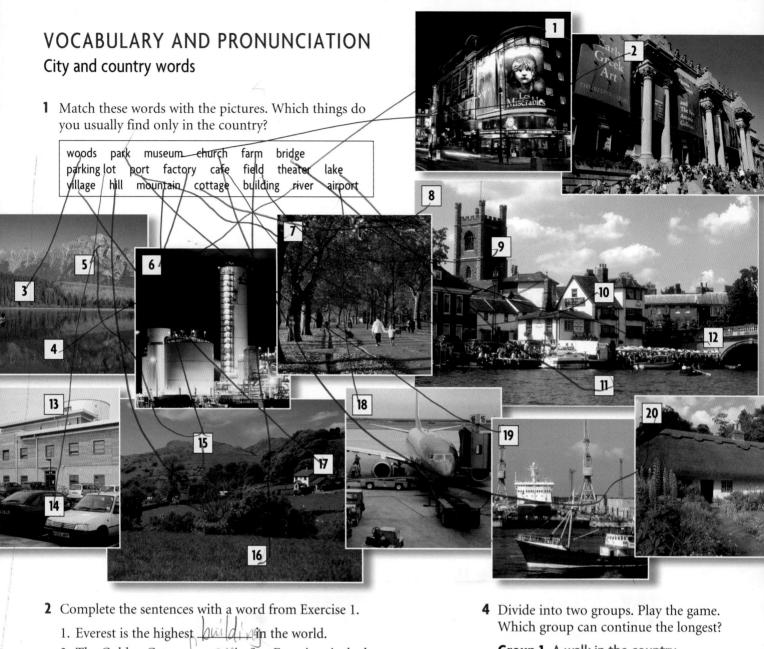

2 Complete the sentences with a word from Exercise 1.

1. Everest is the highest _building_ in the world.
2. The Golden Gate _farm_ in San Francisco is the longest _village_ in the U.S.
3. The Caspian Sea isn't a sea. It's the largest _____ in the world.
4. Singapore is the busiest _airport_ in Asia. Ships from all over the world stop there.
5. The Empire State _building_ in New York was the tallest _parking lot_ in the world for over 40 years.

CD3 33 Listen and check.

3 Write these words from Exercise 1.

/wʊdz/ _____   /fɑrm/ _____   /ˈfæktəri/ _____
/fild/ _____   /ˈθɪətər/ _____   /ˈbrɪdʒ/ _____
/maʊntn/ _____   /tʃɜrtʃ/ _____   /ˈbɪldɪŋ/ _____

CD3 34 Listen and repeat.

4 Divide into two groups. Play the game. Which group can continue the longest?

Group 1 A walk in the country
Continue one after the other.

> I went for a walk in the country and I saw a farm.

> I went for a walk in the country and I saw a farm and some cows.

> I went for ...

Group 2 A walk in the city
Continue one after the other.

> I went for a walk in the city and I saw some stores.

> I went for a walk in the city and I saw some stores and a park.

> I went for ...

EVERYDAY ENGLISH

At the airport

1 What do you do at an airport? Read the sentences and put them in the correct order.

6 You wait in the departure lounge.
7 You board the plane.
2 You get a cart for your luggage.
1 You arrive at the airport.

3 You check in your luggage and get a boarding pass.
4 You go through passport control.
5 You check the departures monitor for your gate number.

2 **CD3 35** Listen to the airport announcements and complete the chart.

FLIGHT NUMBER		DESTINATION	GATE NUMBER	REMARKS
United	8 2 3	S E A T T L E	1 4	N O W B O A R D I N G
American	510	L O S A N G E L E S	10	D E L A Y E D
Northwest	726	D E T R O I T	4	N O W B O A R D I N G
Air Canada	980	W I N N I P E G	7	N O W B O A R D I N G
Delta	169	A T L A N T A	chan	S T A N D B Y

3 **CD3 36** Listen to the conversations. Who are the people? What are they doing?

- meeting people
- checking in luggage
- waiting in the departure lounge
- saying good-bye

4 Complete each conversation with the correct question.

> When can we see each other again?
> Did you have a good honeymoon?
> Did the announcement say gate 4 or 14?
> And carry-on luggage?

1.
A Listen! . . . United flight 823 to Seattle. That's our flight.
B _____ ?
A I couldn't hear. I think it said 14.
B Look! There it is on the monitor. It *is* gate 14.
A OK. Come on! Let's go.

2.
A Can I have your ticket, please?
B Yes, of course.
A Thank you. How many suitcases do you have?
B Just one.
A _____ ?
B Just this bag.
A That's fine.
B Oh . . . can I have a window seat?
A Sure . . . OK. Here's your boarding pass. Have a nice flight!

3.
A Ryan! Tara! Over here!
B Hi! Amy! Great to see you!
A It's great to see you, too. You look terrific!
B _____ ?
B Fantastic. Everything was great.
A Well, you haven't missed anything here. Nothing much has happened at all!

4.
A Well, that's my flight. It's time to go.
B Oh no! It's been a wonderful two weeks. I can't believe it's over.
A I know.
_____ ?
B Soon, I hope. I'll e-mail every day.
A I'll call, too. Good-bye.
B Good-bye. Give my love to your family.

CD3 36 Listen again and check. Work with a partner. Choose a conversation from Exercise 4. Learn it by heart. Pay attention to stress and intonation. Act it out for the class.

▶▶ **WRITING** Writing an e-mail *p. 103*

Writing

UNIT 7 DESCRIBING A VACATION

1 Read the information about Jim and Amy. Make notes about your last vacation.

Questions	Jim	Amy	Me
Where/go?	Vermont	Japan	
When/go?	last June	last October	
How long/stay?	a week	three weeks	
How/travel?	train	plane	
Where/stay?	a bed and breakfast	with friends	
What/do?	went walking in the countryside	visited Tokyo and Kyoto	
What/see?	some beautiful mountains and rivers; *not* any people!	some beautiful temples; *not* Mount Fuji	
Enjoy the vacation?	Yes	Yes	

2 Ask and answer the questions about Jim with a partner.

> Where did he go?
> To Vermont.
> How long did he stay?
> For a week.

3 Complete the questions about Amy and write short answers.

1. Where _____ **did she go** _____ ?   To Japan.
2. When _____ ?   _____
3. How long _____ ?   _____
4. How _____ ?   _____
5. Where _____ ?   _____
6. What _____ ?   _____
7. What _____ ?   _____
8. Did _____ ?   Yes, she did.

4 Read about Amy's vacation. Put the verbs in the Past Simple.

My exciting vacation

Last October I (1) _____ (have) a very exciting vacation. I (2) _____ (go) to Japan for three weeks to stay with friends. I (3) _____ (travel) by plane. It (4) _____ (be) a long trip, but fortunately my friends (5) _____ (meet) me at the airport and (6) _____ (drive) me straight to their house. I (7) _____ (stay) with my friends for the first week. The second week I (8) _____ (visit) Tokyo. The third week I (9) _____ (take) the train to Kyoto where I (10) _____ (see) some beautiful temples and gardens. I (11) _____ (enjoy) the vacation very much, but I (12) _____ (not see) Mount Fuji. Next time I want to climb it with my friends.

5 Talk to a partner about your last vacation. Then write about it.

1 Make sentences with a line in **A**, a word in **B**, and a line in **C**.

A	B	C
1. I left the party early		a. she was thirty.
2. Peter couldn't speak		b. they came for dinner.
3. Tim didn't see the canals	because	c. I was at school.
4. Eva didn't start learning English	when	d. she couldn't afford them.
5. I didn't enjoy math class	until	e. after midnight.
6. Courtney didn't buy the red shoes		f. he was nearly four.
7. They didn't go to bed		g. I didn't feel well.
8. We met Ken's wife last Saturday		h. he was in Bangkok.

2 Write notes about an old friend. Use these questions to help.

- What is his/her name?
- Where did you meet?
- What did you do together?
- How often do you meet now?
- What do you do when you meet?

Talk to a partner about your notes.

3 Read the text about "My oldest friend." Complete the text with words from the box.

| and but because so when until |

My oldest friend

My oldest friend is named Sandra. We met 30 years ago (1) _____ we were both five years old. It was my first day at school (2) _____ I was very unhappy (3) _____ I wanted my mom. Sandra gave me candy (4) _____ we became friends immediately. We were together nearly every day (5) _____ we finished school twelve years later.

Then I went to college, (6) _____ Sandra didn't. She married (7) _____ she was just 18 (8) _____ had three children. I studied for eight years (9) _____ I wanted to be an accountant. I had a lot of new friends, (10) _____ I didn't see Sandra very often. Sometimes we didn't meet for months, (11) _____ we often talked on the telephone.

Now I'm married, too. I live near Sandra (12) _____ we meet every week. She's a student now, (13) _____ I have a baby, (14) _____ we can give each other a lot of advice!

4 Write about your friend. Use your notes to help.

1 Read the e-mail.

- Who is it from?
- What is it about?
- Who is it to?
- How does it begin and end?

2 These lines are from the e-mail. Where do they go?

a. Could you tell me what time the restaurant closes?

b. I look forward to hearing from you.

c. Could I possibly have a quiet room away from the pool?

From: p.west@teleport.net
To: bookings@bluesea.com
Date: March 17
Subject: **Booking a room**

Dear Sir or Madam,

I would like to book a deluxe room at your hotel for the nights of April 12, 13, and 14.
(1)_____

I understand you have a restaurant.
(2)_____

My details are: 15 Carlton Street, Dallas, TX 75201. Tel: (214) 566-4945. Please let me know if you need a deposit or a credit card number.

Thank you very much.
(3)_____

Sincerely,

Peter West

3 Look at the hotel's online booking form. Complete the form with information about Peter West in Exercise 1.

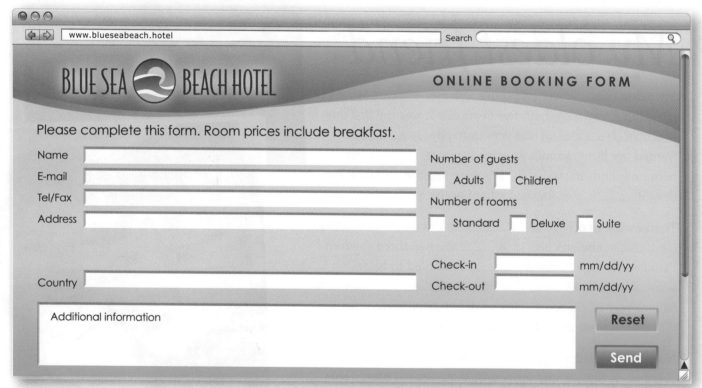

www.blueseabeach.hotel   Search

BLUE SEA BEACH HOTEL   ONLINE BOOKING FORM

Please complete this form. Room prices include breakfast.

Name _____   Number of guests
E-mail _____   ☐ Adults ☐ Children
Tel/Fax _____   Number of rooms
Address _____   ☐ Standard ☐ Deluxe ☐ Suite

Country _____   Check-in ☐ mm/dd/yy
                                            Check-out ☐ mm/dd/yy

Additional information   **Reset**

                                                          Send

4 Write an e-mail to book a room at the hotel.

- Book a standard room for four nights next month.
- Ask for a room with a view of the ocean.
- Ask about Internet and other facilities (phone, television, room service, parking, etc.).
- Give your personal details.

These two sentences have the same meaning. How are they different? Which is more formal?

I like him a lot, but I don't love him.
Although I like him a lot, I don't love him.

1 Complete the sentences with a word from the box.

> although because but
> too both for example

1. My father loves skiing, __*but*__ my mother hates it.

2. We stopped playing tennis _____ it started to rain.

3. _____ it was cold and wet, we still played tennis.

4. My two sisters are very similar. They _____ love dancing and skiing.

5. Rosa loves dancing and Hannah loves it _____ .

6. There's so much to do on weekends. _____ you can go skiing or swimming.

2 Complete the text with the correct linking word from Exercise 1.

3 Work with a partner. Talk about your brothers, sisters, parents, or children. Are you/they similar? Do you/they like doing the same things?

4 Write about two people in your family and compare them. Describe …

- what they look like
- their likes and dislikes
- their personalities

My brother and sister

I have a brother Ben, and a sister Ana. They are a lot younger than me, and (1) _althouqh_ they are twins, they don't look alike at all. Ben has red hair, (2)_____ Ana's hair is blonde. They (3)_____ have blue eyes, (4)_____ Ben is much taller than Ana. They are interested in different things (5)_____. (6)_____, Ben likes numbers and letters, but Ana prefers painting and drawing.

(7)_____ they are so different, there are still some things that they (8)_____ like doing. (9)_____, they love coming into my room and playing with my things, (10)_____ they think my things are much more interesting than theirs!

(11)_____ they are sometimes really noisy and annoying, I love them very much (12)_____ they are so funny.

1 Discuss these questions with a partner.

- Do you often receive postcards? Who from? Where from? Give examples.
- What was the last postcard you sent? Who to? Where from?

2 Read the postcard. Find words for good weather and bad weather.

3 Underline the descriptions for a good vacation *or* a bad vacation. Read your postcard to your partner.

Friday, June 14th

Dear Mom and Dad,

We're having | a wonderful / a pretty good | time here in Puerto Rico, | and fortunately / but unfortunately | the weather is | great / not very good |. They say that the weather here in June is often very changeable so we're | just unlucky / very lucky |. It is | warm and sunny / wet and cloudy | nearly every day, so most of the time we | stay in the hotel / go to the beach | and | play cards / swim and sunbathe |. Yesterday it was so | hot / rainy | that we couldn't | see the sea / lie in the sun |. Tomorrow we're not going to | the beach / stay in the hotel |, we're going to drive around the island and go sightseeing.

See you soon

Love,   Laura and Mike

Mr. and Mrs. Binchey
82 Hill Road
Dublin
Ireland

Puerto Rico

4 Write a postcard to a friend. Write about …

- where you are on vacation
- the weather
- something you do often
- something you did yesterday
- something you are going to do tomorrow

1 Have you ever been to another country to study the language? Where did you go? For how long? What language did you study? Did you have a good time?

2 Do you remember So-young who went to study English in New York City? Look quickly at the e-mail.

- Where is So-young now?
- Where are they?
- Who is Jae-sun?
- Who is she writing to?
- Why is she writing?

3 Read the e-mail again and complete it with the words from the box. Check with a partner.

lot	going x2	couldn't
visit	just	has
quickly	much	but
had	like	

From:	So-young@kmail.kr
To:	Becky@teleport.net
Date:	October 23
Subject:	Hi!

Dear Becky and family,

I have (1) _____ arrived back in Korea. It's nice to see my family again (2) _____ I miss you and all my friends in New York. I (3) _____ a wonderful time with you and your family. I enjoyed myself very (4) _____ . Also, it was very nice of you to show me so much of the city. I loved (5) _____ to Central Park, and I'll never forget visiting the Empire State Building and the Statue of Liberty.

I think that my English (6) _____ improved a (7) _____ . At first I was so worried because I (8) _____ understand a word. You all spoke so (9) _____ , but soon I began to understand more and more.

My brother, Jae-sun, is (10) _____ to New York City next month. Can he come to see you? He'd (11) _____ to very much. I hope that one day you can (12) _____ me in Korea. I would love to show you Seoul.

Love to you all,
So-young

4 Write a similar e-mail to someone you have stayed with.

Audio Scripts

UNIT 7

CD2 20

A Who is she?
Oprah Winfrey is a famous American TV talk show host. Forty-nine million people in 134 countries watch her show every week. She lives in California but she also has an apartment in Chicago, where she works. Oprah is one of the richest women in America. She earns millions of dollars every year. She gives a lot of money to charity.

CD2 21 see p. 48

CD2 22

watch/watched	earn/earned
talk/talked	open/opened
move/moved	study/studied
interview/interviewed	start/started

CD2 23

C Oprah the TV star
In 1984 Oprah moved to Chicago to work on a TV talk show called *A.M. Chicago*. She talked to lots of interesting people about their problems. Oprah says, "People's problems are my problems." The show was very successful, so in 1985 it was renamed *The Oprah Winfrey Show*. In 1993 she interviewed Michael Jackson and 100 million people watched the program. Last year she earned $260,000,000.

In 1998 Oprah started the charity Oprah's Angel Network. This helps poor children all over the world. In 2007 she opened a special school in South Africa, the Oprah Winfrey Leadership Academy for Girls. She says, "When I was a kid, we were poor and we didn't have much money. So what did I do? I studied hard." There are 152 girls at the school, Oprah calls them her daughters—the children she didn't have in real life.

CD2 24

1. A Where did her father work?
   B In a coal mine.
2. A What did her mother do?
   B She cleaned houses.
3. A Who did Oprah live with?
   B Her grandmother.
4. A What did she study?
   B Drama.
5. A When did she interview Michael Jackson?
   B In 1993.
6. A How much did she earn last year?
   B $260 million.
7. A When did she open the girls school?
   B In 2007.
8. A Did her parents earn much money?
   B No, they didn't.

CD2 25 see p. 50

CD2 26

wanted	danced
loved	retired
acted	earned
looked	liked

CD2 27

beat	hit
became	invented
began	left
bought	made
came	sold
got	sang
went	won
had	

CD2 28

1989 The year I was born
J=James, D=Dad, M=Mom
J   Dad, tell me about the year I was born. I know you and mom were in Brazil. You had a job there, didn't you?
D   Yes, that's right. You were born in January, and we left Brazil in April and . . .
J   . . . and you went back to the States.
D   Yes, we did. I got a job in New York.
M   Yes. The first Bush was President then. Do you remember Robert? He was the father of George W. Bush, James.
J   I know that, Mom. Who else was in power then?
D   Well,—um—in Russia Mikhail Gorbachev became President of the Soviet Union and . . .
M   Oh yes, It was the time of the Cold War. Did you know that James?
J   No, I didn't, Mom!
D   Yeah, but 1989 was the year the Cold War ended and everything changed.
M   That's for sure. The Berlin Wall came down between East and West Germany and the world changed. It was an exciting time.
D   Yeah, 1989 was exciting—in sports too, James. In October the Oakland A's beat the San Francisco Giants in the baseball World Series. But do you know a huge earthquake hit San Francisco right before Game Three started.
J   No way! Did they stop the game?
D   They did. They finished it twelve days later. Sixty-seven people died in the earthquake.
J   That's terrible.
M   Sure was. Now, what else happened in '89? Weren't computers big news?
J   Computers were new?
D   No, no, a lot of people had computers. But the Internet was born in '89—a guy called Tim Berners-Lee invented the World Wide Web. He won $1.5 million for doing that.

M   Oh, and James, you like video games. Nintendo began selling Game Boy in '89. They sold 30 million in just three years.
J   Wow! What else? I mean, what did people watch on TV?
D   Well, the Simpsons made their television debut. Mom and I didn't like them at first but now . . .
J   And what about music? Who was famous back then?
D   Let me think. Some bands you know: Depeche Mode, R.E.M., New Kids on the Block . . .
M   Oh, and Madonna sang "Like a Prayer," I loved that. We bought the album.
J   Wow, that's amazing! She's still famous today. Hey, it was a good year, the year I was born.

CD2 29

orange juice	movie star
train station	birthday card
swimming pool	washing machine
handbag	living room
boyfriend	parking lot
newspaper	

CD2 30

1. A I can't find my handbag.
   B Here it is!
   A Oh, thank you. Where did you find it?
   B In the living room where you left it!
2. A Would you like some chocolate cake?
   B No, thanks, just orange juice for me.
   A But I made this cake for you.
   B Did you? I'm sorry! I don't like chocolate cake.
3. A I have nothing to wear for your boyfriend's party.
   B What about your white jeans?
   A They aren't clean.
   B Well, wash them. You have a washing machine, don't you?
4. A Do you want anything from the store?
   B A newspaper, please. *The New York Times*, I think.
   A OK.
   B Oh, and can you take this letter to the post office?
   A Sure.

CD2 31

first	thirteenth
second	sixteenth
third	seventeenth
fourth	twentieth
fifth	twenty-first
sixth	thirtieth
tenth	thirty-first
twelfth	

1. April first
2. March second
3. September seventeenth
4. November nineteenth
5. June twenty-third
6. February twenty-ninth, nineteen seventy-six
7. December nineteenth, nineteen eighty-three
8. October third, nineteen ninety-nine
9. May thirty-first, two thousand
10. July fifteenth, two thousand and seven

CD2 | 33

1. January fourth
2. May seventh, 1997
3. August fifteenth, 2001
4. A   It was a Friday.
   B   No, it wasn't. It was a Thursday.
   A   No, I remember. It was Friday the thirteenth. July thirteenth.
5. A   Oh no! I forgot your birthday.
   B   It's OK, really.
   A   It was last Sunday, wasn't it? The thirtieth. November thirtieth.
6. A   Hey! Did you know that Shakespeare was born and died on the same day?
   B   No way!
   A   Yes. He was born on April twenty-third, fifteen sixty-four, and he died on April twenty-third, sixteen sixteen.

UNIT 8

CD2 | 34

The photograph
Louis Daguerre from France
Louis Daguerre was a painter for the French opera. But he wanted to make a new type of picture. He started his experiments in the 1820s. Twelve years later he invented the photograph. He sold his idea to the French government in 1839 and the government gave it to the world. Daguerre called the first photographs "daguerreotypes." They became popular very fast. By 1850, there were 70 daguerreotype studios in New York City.

The windshield wiper
Mary Anderson from the United States
Mary Anderson often visited New York City by car. In winter she noticed that when it rained or snowed, drivers got out of their cars all the time to clean their windows. In 1903 she began designing something to clean windows from inside the car. People, especially men, laughed at her idea. But they didn't laugh for long. She invented the windshield wiper in 1905. And by 1916 all American cars had them.

The bicycle
Kirkpatrick Macmillan from Scotland
Long ago in 1490, Leonardo da Vinci drew a design for the modern bicycle. But the first person to make a bicycle was Kirkpatrick Macmillan in 1839. He lived in Scotland, so people didn't hear about his invention for a long time. Twenty years later, another bicycle came

from France. In 1895 the bike became cheap and everyone could have one. Now people, especially women, could travel to the next town. It helped them find someone to marry!

CD2 | 35

1. He didn't invent the bicycle. He invented the photograph.
2. He didn't give his idea to the French government. He sold it to them.
3. She didn't live in New York City. She often visited New York City.
4. All cars didn't have windshield wipers by 1916. Only American cars had them.
5. Leonardo da Vinci didn't make the first bicycle. Kirkpatrick Macmillan made it.
6. He didn't come from France. He came from Scotland.

CD2 | 36   see p. 58

CD2 | 37   see p. 59

CD2 | 38

1. white
2. bought
3. night
4. answer
5. building
6. Christmas

CD2 | 39   see p. 59

CD2 | 40

He's not your type!
C=Claudia, N=Neil
C   A year ago, I had a boyfriend named Stuart, I thought he was OK but my friends didn't like him. You know how it goes, "Claudia, Stuart's just so not your type. He's boring." So, what did I do? I broke up with him. And as soon as we broke up, my friends posted my picture on a dating website.
N   Yeah, and that's when I first saw Claudia.
C   But my friends didn't tell me—I mean, I didn't know anything about the website picture! They said they knew I could meet someone better than Stuart.
N   Well, it was lucky for me that Claudia's friends posted her picture. I saw it and wrote to her.
C   Yeah, I started receiving lots of e-mails from people I didn't know. I couldn't understand it! Most of them went into my junk mailbox and I deleted them.
N   But you didn't delete mine. My e-mail went into Claudia's Inbox.
C   Yeah, somehow Neil's got through and I opened it. And for some reason I couldn't stop thinking about him. It was strange because I usually don't meet people online.
N   Well, I didn't know that.
C   So, anyway, he asked me out for a cup of coffee …
N   … we met in Starbucks and immediately …
C   Yeah, immediately everything just clicked. I know it sounds like a movie or something, but it was fantastic. We talked and laughed a lot. By the end of the date we just knew.
N   I guess your friends were right, huh?
C   That's for sure! Poor Stuart, he wasn't my type at all.

Do mothers know best?
E=Eric, L=Lori
E   Our story is easy. We didn't do anything. It was our mothers who did it all!
L   Yes. You see, our mothers are friends. They met one summer by the lake. They both have little summer houses there. And, of course, they talked a lot about their children.
E   … and they decided that they wanted us to meet.
L   We both thought this wasn't a very good idea!
E   When my mom said to me "I know a nice girl for you," I just thought, "No way."
L   Me, too! You see, my mom did this a lot, and it was usually terrible.
E   But we finally said "OK"—just for some peace.
L   I took my sister with me …
E   … and I took my best friend, Steve.
L   But I was so surprised! Eric was wonderful!
E   And of course, I thought the same about Lori. We all had a great time by the lake that summer. And at the end of the summer I knew I was in love with Lori.
L   That was four years ago, and our wedding is in the fall. Our mothers are very happy, and we are, too!
E   Yes. Sometimes mothers know best!

CD2 | 41   Song: Teacher's Book p. 120

CD2 | 42

1. Happy birthday to you.
   Happy birthday to you.
   Happy birthday, dear Grandma,
   Happy birthday to you.
2. A   Did you get any Valentine cards?
   B   Yes, I did. Listen to this.
       Roses are red. Violets are blue.
       You are my Valentine
       And I love you.
   A   Wow! Do you know who it's from?
   B   No idea!
3. A   Wake up, Mommy! Happy Mother's Day!
   B   Thank you. Oh, what beautiful flowers, and a cup of coffee!
   A   And I made you a card! Look!
   B   It's beautiful. What a sweet boy!
4. A   Congratulations!
   B   Thank you very much!
   A   When's the big day?
   B   Excuse me?
   A   When's your wedding day?
   B   June 26th. Didn't you get your invitation?
5. A   It's midnight! Happy New Year everybody!
   B   Happy New Year!
   C   Happy New Year!
6. A   Thank goodness! It's Friday!
   B   Yeah. Have a nice weekend!
   A   Same to you.
7. A   Ugh! Work again. I hate Monday mornings!
   B   Me, too. Did you have a good weekend?
   A   Yes, I did. It was great.

UNIT 9

CD3 2

D = Daisy, T = Tom

D Mmm, I love apple juice. Do you like it Tom?
T No—it's disgusting. I like soda, ... and I love coffee.
D Yuck! You don't! You don't drink coffee!
T Yes, I do. Sometimes my dad gives me some of his coffee—and I love it.
D Well, that's different ... My dad drinks coffee—I don't like coffee at all. But my mom drinks tea and I love tea.
T No, I don't like tea, but I like orange juice. It's funny—I like orange juice, but I don't like oranges. I don't like fruit very much at all. Except bananas—I really like bananas.
D Really? I like all fruit—apples, oranges, bananas, and I love strawberries. And ... what about vegetables, do you like them?
T No—I don't eat vegetables.
D What? Never? Not even potatoes? You eat french fries—I know you do.
T Yeah—OK, I eat potatoes—especially french fries. French fries and hamburgers. I love that for dinner.
D I don't like hamburgers—my favorite dinner is pasta with peas.
T Peas—yuck!
D I like vegetables—especially carrots and peas, oh, and tomatoes. Hey, are tomatoes fruit or vegetable?
T I don't know. Anyway, I don't like tomatoes—except on pizza with cheese. I love pizza.
D Me, too.
T Anyway, I know your favorite food.
D No, you don't!
T Yes, I do. It's chocolate—all girls like chocolate!
D Boys like chocolate too! You ate all those chocolate chip cookies at my house last week.
T They were cookies. That's different. Anyway—you ate more than me ...
D No, I didn't!
T Yes, you did!
D Didn't!
T Did!

CD3 3 see p. 63

CD3 4

1. Would you like a tuna salad sandwich?
   No, thanks. I'm not hungry.
2. Do you like Ella?
   Yes. She's very nice.
3. Would you like a cold drink?
   Yes, soda, please.
4. Can I help you?
   Yes. I'd like some stamps, please.
5. What sports do you do?
   Well, I like swimming very much.
6. Excuse me, are you ready to order?
   Yes. I'd like a steak, please.

CD3 5

1. Good afternoon. Can I help you?
2. Who's your favorite writer?
3. What would you like for your birthday?
4. Do you like animals?
5. Here's the menu, sir.
6. Have some ice cream with your strawberries.

CD3 6

1. A Good afternoon. Can I help you?
   B Yes. I'd like some fruit, please.
2. A Who's your favorite writer?
   B I like books by John Grisham.
3. A What would you like for your birthday?
   B I'd like a new bike.
4. A Do you like animals?
   B I like cats, but I don't like dogs.
5. A Here's the menu, sir.
   B I'd like a plate of pasta.
6. A Have some ice cream with your strawberries.
   B No, thanks. I don't like ice cream.

CD3 7

At the market

M = Mom, T = Tom, V = Vendor

M Tom! Hurry up!
T Aw, Mom, I don't like shopping.
M Come on, Tom. I need your help.
T OK.
....
V Good morning Ma'am. How can I help you today?
M Well, I'd like some apple juice, please.
V How many bottles?
M Two, please.
T But Mom, ... I don't like apple juice.
M Shh Tom. It's good for you. Thank you. Here ... You can carry them.
T Oh no!
M And some tomatoes, please.
V No problem. These tomatoes are very fresh. There we are.
M And I'd like some of that cheddar cheese, please.
V This one? How much? Is this much OK?
M That's fine, thanks. And ... is there any whole wheat bread? I can't see any.
V Sorry, no, there isn't—but there's some nice white bread. Look! It's homemade.
M Ummm. ...
T Mom, I really like white bread. Please can we have it?
M Oh, OK then. Yes, thanks.
V Anything else?
T Oh yeah! Mom! Look at those cakes!
M Shh Tom. ... Um ... oh yes, some apples.
V How many—one bag or two?
M Two bags, please.
T Oh yuck. Can't we have bananas?
M No, we can't. Here. Take these bags for me.
T Oh Mom! They're heavy!
M Thanks. ... How much is all that?
V Let's see, that's ten dollars and eighty-five cents.
M Here you are.
V Thanks. And here's your change.

M Thanks. Bye!
....
T Phew! Is that everything?
M No, ummm, ... I still need ummm ...
T Mom, not more. I hate shopping!
M ... need to buy your new sneakers, but if you don't want to ...
T New sneakers—cool!
M ... But I thought you didn't like shopping ...
T Yeah, but ...

CD3 8

My favorite national food

Danupol

One dish that is very famous in my country is the pad thai. It's rice noodles mixed with eggs, chili sauce, garlic, and peanuts. Some people like to make it with chicken or pork, but I like it with shrimp! You can find it in many restaurants around the world, but the best pad thai is made by street vendors in Thailand. When I'm back home in Bangkok I always go to my favorite pad thai place and order it with extra fish sauce and lime. Mmmm!

Natalie

Now in my job, I travel the world, and I like all kinds of food ... but my favorite, my favorite is ... um ... I always have it as soon as I come home ... is a big American breakfast. Bacon, eggs, sausage, and of course, pancakes. I love it, not every day, but when I'm at home we have it every Sunday. Mmmm! I'd like it right now. Delicious.

Giulia

We love eating in my country! One of my favorite national dishes is called "bruschetta." This is actually toast, but you make it with special bread. You can eat it with a lot of things, but my favorite bruschetta has tomatoes, garlic, and olive oil on it. In my town there is a "bruschetteria." This is a small cafe—selling only toast! It's my favorite place to go.

Sergio

One kind of food that my country is very famous for is meat, especially beef. Everybody eats a lot of meat here. My family eats beef three or four times a week. There are a lot of different beef dishes, but my favorite is "bife de chorizo." This is a big steak! My mom cooks it with tomatoes and chili peppers. Delicious!

CD3 9

1. Would you like some more carrots?
   Yes, please. They're delicious.
2. Could you pass the salt, please?
   Yes, of course. Here you are.
3. Could I have a glass of water, please?
   Do you want bottled water or tap water?
4. Does anybody want more bread?
   Yes, please. I'd love some.
5. How would you like your coffee?
   Black, no sugar, please.
6. This is delicious! Can you give me the recipe?
   Yes, of course. I'm glad you like it.
7. Do you want help with the dishes?
   No, of course not. We have a dishwasher.

CD3 | 10 see p. 69

CD3 | 11

1. A Can I have a cheese sandwich, please?
   B Yes, of course. That's $1.75.
2. A Could you tell me the time, please?
   B It's just after ten.
3. A Can you take me to the station, please?
   B Jump in.
4. A Can I see the menu, please?
   B Here you are. And would you like a drink to start?
5. A Could you lend me some money, please?
   B Not again! How much would you like this time?
6. A Can you help me with my homework, please?
   B What is it? Spanish? I can't speak a word of Spanish.
7. A Can I borrow your dictionary, please?
   B Yes, if I can find it. I think it's in my bag.

UNIT 10

CD3 | 12

Who's at the wedding?
A=Alan, M=Mike
A Mike, I don't know any of these people. Who are they?
M Can you see that man over there? He's sitting down. That's my uncle George. He's an architect. He works in L.A.
A Sorry, where?
M You know, L.A. Los Angeles.
A Oh, yes.
M And he's talking to James. He's wearing a blue shirt. He teaches math at a school in San Francisco.
A He's a teacher?
M Yes, that's right. Next to him is Fiona. She's drinking a cup of coffee. Fiona's my cousin.
A And what does Fiona do?
M She's a writer. She writes children's stories. She's talking to Sue. Sue's wearing a red dress. She works in a hospital. She's a nurse.
A And who are those two over there? They're eating cake.
M Oh, that's Bill and John. They went to school with me. They live in Seattle now. Bill is wearing a pink shirt and John is wearing a green shirt.
A So, ummm … that's George and James and … uh … it's no good, I can't remember all those names.

CD3 | 13

1. A Whose baseball cap is this?
   B It's his.
2. A Whose flowers are these?
   B They're hers.
3. A Whose dog is this?
   B It's theirs.

CD3 | 14

1. Who's on the phone?
2. I'm going to the mall. Who's coming?
3. Wow! Look at that sports car. Whose is it?
4. A Whose dictionary is this?
   B It's not mine.
5. There are books all over the floor. Whose are they?
6. Who's the most intelligent in our class?
7. Do you know whose jacket this is?

CD3 | 15

A Whose tennis racket is this?
B It's mine.
A What's it doing here?
B I'm playing tennis this afternoon.

CD3 | 16

1. A Whose sunglasses are these?
   B They're John's. He's going to the beach later.
2. A Whose shoes are these?
   B They're Mary's. She's going dancing tonight.
3. A Whose suitcase is this?
   B It's mine. I'm going on vacation tomorrow.
4. A Whose coat is this?
   B It's Jane's. She's going for a walk soon.
5. A Whose plane ticket is this?
   B It's Jo's. She's flying to Houston this afternoon.
6. A Whose glasses are these?
   B They're ours. We're having a party tonight.

CD3 | 17

"Flying Without Wings"
Everybody's looking for that something
One thing that makes it all complete
You find it in the strangest places
Places you never knew it could be
Some find it in the faces of their children
Some find it in their lover's eyes
Who can deny the joy it brings
When you find that special thing
You're flying without wings
Some find it sharing every morning
Some in their solitary lives
You find it in the words of others
A simple line can make you laugh or cry
You find it in the deepest friendship
The kind you cherish all your life
And when you know how much that means
You've found that special thing
You're flying without wings
So impossible as it may seem
You've got to fight for every dream
'Cause who's to know which one you let go
Would have made you complete
Well, for me it's waking up beside you
To watch the sunrise on your face
To know that I can say I love you

At any given time or place
It's little things that only I know
Those are the things that make you mine
And it's like flying without wings
'Cause you're my special thing
I'm flying without wings
You're the place my life begins
And you'll be where it ends
I'm flying without wings
And that's the joy you bring
I'm flying without wings

CD3 | 18

SP Can I help you?
C Yes, please. I'm looking for a shirt to go with my new jeans.
SP What color are you looking for?
C Blue.
SP What about this one? Do you like this?
C No, it isn't the right blue.
SP Well, what about this one? It's a bit darker blue.
C Oh yes. I like that one much better. Can I try it on?
SP Yes, of course. The fitting rooms are over there.
. . .
SP Is the size OK?
C No, it's a bit too big. Do you have a smaller size?
SP That's the last blue one we have, I'm afraid. But we have it in green.
C OK. I'll take the green. How much is it?
SP $39.99. How do you want to pay?
C Can I pay by credit card?
SP Credit card's fine. Thank you very much.

UNIT 11

CD3 19

Future plans

Jack

When I grow up I'm going to be a soccer player—a really good one. I'm on the school team and I play three times a week. But I'm going to train very hard, every day, so I can be really, really good. First I'm going to play for a Major League Soccer team. Then I'm going to travel all over the world and I'm going to be famous. I'm not going to marry until I'm very old—about 25. Then I want to have two sons. I'm going to play soccer until I'm 35—that's a very long time. And I'm going to teach my sons to play. I want them to be famous soccer players, too!

Danny Carrick

When I retire next year ... I'm going to retire early ... I'm not going to stay at home and watch TV. I'm going to try lots of new things. First I want to go mountain climbing. In fact, I want to climb Mount Everest, so I'm going to train very hard for that. I'm going to learn to scuba dive, too, because I want to go scuba diving in Australia. There are so many things I want to do! I'm going to travel all over the world, then I'm going to write a book about my adventures. I want to call it *Life Begins at 60!* In my book, I'm going to tell other retired people to try new things, too. You are only as old as you feel!

CD3 20 see p. 78

CD3 21

1. A Why is he going to train very hard?
   B Because he wants to be a soccer player.
2. A How long is he going to play soccer?
   B Until he's 35.
3. A When is he going to marry?
   B Not until he's very old—about 25!
4. A How many children is he going to have?
   B Two.
5. A Who is he going to teach to play?
   B His sons.

CD3 22

T=Tony, A=Amanda
T So, what would you like to do this year, Amanda?
A What about a beach vacation? That's relaxing.
T Uh! Relaxing and boring! What about a ski trip?
A Too dangerous and stressful for me—and expensive.
T Well, what about camping in Arizona? Camping is cheaper and safer than skiing.
A Mmmm. Actually, what I'd really like is a week in New York, going sightseeing. New York is such an exciting city.
T Mmmm! Exciting, yes, but more expensive than other vacations.

CD3 23

1. A I think a vacation in Los Angeles is cheaper than a vacation in Miami.
   B I don't think so. Los Angeles is much more expensive.

2. A I think Boston is smaller and older than New York.
   B Well, you're right, Boston *is* smaller, but it's *not* older.
3. A A ski trip is going to be more exciting than hiking in the mountains.
   B I don't agree. Hiking is much more exciting.
4. A I think mountain climbing is much more dangerous than sky diving.
   B Really? I think they're both very frightening. I don't think one is safer than the other.
5. A Which city do you think is better, Mexico City or Buenos Aires?
   B I don't know. I think they're both great. I don't think one is more exciting than the other.

CD3 24

1. A Mount Everest is a very big mountain.
   B Yes, it's the biggest mountain in the world. Did you know that it's 8,850 meters high?
2. A The Lakers are a very famous basketball team.
   B Yes, I think they're the best team in the world. I think they're going to win the NBA title this year.
3. A The Ritz is a very expensive hotel.
   B Yes, it's one of the most expensive hotels in the city.
4. A New York's a very cosmopolitan city.
   B Yes, it's one of the most cosmopolitan cities in the world. London's also very cosmopolitan.
5. A Brad Pitt is a very popular movie star.
   B Yes, he's one of the most popular movie stars in America, but I don't like him. Do you?
6. A Miss Smith is a very funny teacher.
   B Yes, she's the funniest teacher in our school. She's the best, too. But it's so sad, she's going to leave soon.
7. A Anna is a very intelligent student.
   B Yes, she's the most intelligent student in the class. She's certainly a lot smarter than I am.
8. A This is a very easy exercise.
   B Yes, it's the easiest in the book. I think they're all pretty easy, don't you?

CD3 25

A What's the weather like today?
B It's snowy and it's very cold.
A What was it like yesterday?
B Oh, it was cold and cloudy.
A What's it going to be like tomorrow?
B I think it's going to be warmer.

CD3 26

1. A It's a beautiful day! What should we do?
   B Let's play tennis!
2. A It's raining again! What should we do?
   B Let's stay at home and watch a DVD.

CD3 27

1. A It's a beautiful day! What should we do?
   B Let's play tennis!
   A Oh no! It's too hot to play tennis.

B Well, let's go to the beach.
A I'll get my bathing suit.
2. A It's raining again! What should we do?
   B Let's stay at home and watch a DVD.
   A But we watched a DVD last night.
   B Well, let's go to the movies.
   A OK. What movie do you want to see?

UNIT 12

CD3 28

S = Steve, R = Ryan
S Ryan, where are you and Tara going for your honeymoon?
R Somewhere in Europe, we think. France, maybe, or Spain. I've been to Paris, but I haven't been to Barcelona.
S Yes, Paris is beautiful. But what about Venice? It's very romantic.
R Mmm, that's an idea. I've been to Italy, but I've never been to Venice.
S What about Tara? Where does she want to go?
R Oh, Tara doesn't mind where we go. She's been to Mexico and Brazil, but she hasn't been anywhere in Europe!

CD3 29 see p. 86

CD3 30 see p. 86

CD3 31

What has Ryan done?

Yes, I've lived in a foreign country—in Japan. I lived in Osaka for a year. I enjoyed it very much. I loved the food. And, yes, I have worked for a big company. I worked for Nissan, the car company, that's why I was in Japan. That was three years ago, then I got a job back in New York.

Have I stayed in an expensive hotel? No, never—only cheap hotels for me, I'm afraid, but I have flown in a jumbo jet—lots of times, actually. Oh, I've never cooked a meal for a lot of people. I love food, but I don't like cooking much. Sometimes I cook for me and my girlfriend Tara, but she likes it better if we go out to eat! And I've never met a famous person—oh, just a minute, well not met, but I've seen ... ummm ... I saw a famous politician at the airport once—oh, who was it? I can't remember his name, um ... I've only seen one Shakespeare play, when I was in high school, we saw *Romeo and Juliet*. It was OK. I've ridden a motorcycle though. My brother has one. It's very fast. Fortunately, I've never been in the hospital. My brother has—he fell off his motorcycle! Unfortunately, I've never won a competition. I play the lottery every week, but I've never, ever won a thing!

CD3 32

A honeymoon in Venice
T = Tara, A = Amy
T We're having a great time!
A Tell me about it! What have you done so far?
T Well, we've been to St. Mark's Square. That was the first thing we did. It's right in the center of Venice. We sat outside in the sun

and had coffee. We've seen the paintings in the Doge's Palace. It was wonderful. But we haven't climbed up St. Mark's Bell Tower yet. It was too busy. We're going early tomorrow morning.

A Have you been in a gondola yet?

T Oh yes, we have! We took a gondola trip yesterday evening. It was so romantic! And we went on a fantastic boat ride along the Grand Canal and we went under the Rialto Bridge! But we haven't walked across it yet. I want to do that.

A Wow! You're busy! Have you visited the Murano glass factories yet? Don't forget—I want a glass horse!

T I haven't forgotten. In fact, we took a boat to Murano island yesterday, and I got your horse. OK?

A Oh, thank you, thank you! So what else are you going to do?

T Well, I'd like to go to the beach, you know—at the Lido. It's so hot here! But we haven't really decided what else to do yet. There's so much to see.

A Oh, you're so lucky! Have a great time. Say hello to Ryan for me!

T Yeah. Bye, Amy. See you next week at the airport!

CD3 33

1. Everest is the highest mountain in the world.
2. The Golden Gate Bridge in San Francisco is the longest bridge in the U.S.
3. The Caspian Sea isn't a sea. It's the largest lake in the world.
4. Singapore is the busiest port in Asia. Ships from all over the world stop there.
5. The Empire State Building in New York was the tallest building in the world for over 40 years.

CD3 34

woods	bridge
farm	mountain
factory	church
field	building
theater	

CD3 35

May I have your attention please? United Airlines flight 823 to Seattle is now boarding at gate 14. Final boarding announcement for United Airlines Flight 823 to Seattle.

American Airlines flight 516 to Los Angeles is delayed for one hour due to weather. We apologize for any inconvenience.

Northwest flight 726 to Detroit is now boarding at gate 4. Northwest flight 726 to Detroit, now boarding, gate 4.

Air Canada flight 98 to Winnipeg is on time and boarding at gate 20.

Delta flight 609 to Atlanta will have a gate change. Please wait in the departure lounge for a further announcement.

Passengers are reminded to keep their carry-on luggage with them at all times. Thank you.

CD3 36

1. **A** Listen! . . . United Flight 823 to Seattle. That's our flight.
   B Did the announcement say gate 4 or 14?
   A I couldn't hear. I think it said 14.
   B Look! There it is on the monitor. It *is* gate 14.
   A OK. Come on! Let's go.

2. **A** Can I have your ticket, please?
   B Yes, of course.
   A Thank you. How many suitcases do you have?
   B Just one.
   A And carry-on luggage?
   B Just this bag.
   A That's fine.
   B Oh . . . can I have a window seat?
   A Sure . . . OK. Here's your boarding pass. Have a nice flight!

3. **A** Ryan! Tara! Over here!
   B Hi! Amy! Great to see you!
   A It's great to see you, too. You look terrific! Did you have a good honeymoon?
   B Fantastic. Everything was great.
   A Well, you haven't missed anything here. Nothing much has happened at all!

4. **A** Well, that's my flight. It's time to go.
   B Oh no! It's been a wonderful two weeks. I can't believe it's over.
   A I know. When can we see each other again?
   B Soon, I hope. I'll e-mail every day.
   A I'll call, too. Good-bye.
   B Good-bye. Give my love to your family.

CD3 37 Song: Teacher's Book p. 126

Grammar Reference

UNIT 7

7.1 Past Simple – spelling of regular verbs ▶ Ex. 1

1. The normal rule is to add -ed.
   worked   started
   If the verb ends in -e, add -d.
   lived   loved

2. If the verb has only one syllable and one vowel and one consonant, double the consonant.
   stopped   planned

3. Verbs that end in a consonant + -y change to -ied.
   studied   carried

7.2 Past Simple ▶ Ex. 1–3

The Past Simple expresses a past action that is finished.
   I **lived** in Seoul when I was six.
   She **started** work when she was eight.
The form of the Past Simple is the same in all persons.

Affirmative

I He/She/It We You They	moved went	to Atlanta in 1995.

Negative

We use *didn't* + infinitive (without *to*) in all persons.

I He/She/It We You They	didn't	move go	to Atlanta.

Question

We use *did* + infinitive (without *to*) in all persons.

When Where	did	I you he/she/it we/they	go?

Yes/No questions

Did	you she they etc.	like enjoy	the movie? the party?

Short answers

No, I didn't.
No, we didn't.
Yes, she did.
No, they didn't.

There is list of irregular verbs on page 133.

7.3 Time expressions ▶ Ex. 4

last	night week Saturday	month year

yesterday	morning afternoon evening

7.4 Prepositions

They talked **about** their problems.
He worked **in** a coal mine.
She worked **for** a radio station.
She went **to** school when she was 20.
She flew **across** the Atlantic.
Are you interested **in** modern art?

EXERCISES

1 Complete the sentences. Use the Past Simple.

1. I _stopped_ playing football at 5 P.M. (stop)
2. She _worked_ in a cafe last summer. (work)
3. You _didn't saw_ John last week. (not see)
4. _went_ they + _went_ to college? (go)
5. Sarah _lived_ in New York in 2002. (live)
6. When _arrived_ he _arrived_? (arrive)
7. Peter _decided_ to travel around Europe. (decide)
8. Luke _had_ two dogs and a cat. (have)
9. When _finished_ the movie _finished_ (finish)
10. They _want_ a vacation in Florida. (want)

2 Write the Past Simple of the verbs.

1. walk — _walked_   6. write — _wrote_
2. go — _went_   7. study — _studed_
3. see — _saw_   8. run — _ran_
4. eat — _ate_   9. sing — _sang_
5. become — _became_   10. hear — _heared_

3 Write short answers that are true for you.

1. Did you watch TV last week? _Yes_
2. Did you and your friends go out last weekend? _Yes_
3. Did your father teach you to ride a bike? _No_
4. Did your parents travel abroad when you were a child? _Yes_

4 Put the time expressions in the correct row.

morning	night	afternoon	year	evening	week

| last | _night_ _year_ _week_ |
| yesterday | _morning_ _afternoon_ _evening_ |

UNIT 8

8.1 Past Simple ▶ Ex. 1–3

Negative

Negatives in the Past Simple are the same in all persons.

I/He/She We/You/They	didn't	go out see Tom	last night.

ago

I went to Brazil	ten years/two weeks/a month	ago.

8.2 Time expressions ▶ Ex. 4

in	the twentieth century/1924/the 1990s winter/summer/the evening/morning/September
on	October 10/Christmas Day/Saturday/Sunday evening
at	seven o'clock/night

8.3 Prepositions

He started **in** the 1820s.
Only U.S. cars had windshield wipers **by** 1916.
I tried to forget **about** him.
People didn't hear **about** his invention.

People laughed **at** her idea.
I fell **in** love **with** him.
They lived **by** the lake.

EXERCISES

1 Make sentences.
1. Sue / yesterday / to the movies / went
   Sue went to the movie yesterday
2. ago / I / met / Nick / two years
   I met Nick two years ago
3. last night / go / they / out / didn't
   They didn't go out last night
4. three weeks / Jack / ago / was born
   Jack was born three weeks
5. Friday / we / last / met
   We met last Friday

2 Rewrite the sentences. Use the negative form of the Past Simple.
1. I watched TV last night. *I didn't watch TV last night*
2. They traveled by train. *They didn't travel by train*
3. Mary sang in the concert last week. *Mary didn't sing in the concert last week*
4. Pete saw three men outside the bank. *Pete didn't see three man outside the bank*
5. We went to New York in 2002. *We didn't travel to New York in 2002*

3 Complete the sentences. Use the Past Simple.
1. Nick *fell* off his bike. (fall)
2. I *sended* them an e-mail. (send)
3. You *finded* my glasses! (find)
4. She *drank* a cup of coffee. (drink)
5. We *bought* a new DVD. (buy)

4 Choose the correct preposition.
1. They met *on / at / in* June 11.
2. Kate was born *in / at / on* the 1980s.
3. We play tennis *on / in / at* weekends.
4. She bought the apartment *at / on / in* May.
5. What did you do *in / at / on* Monday?

UNIT 9

9.1 Count and noncount nouns ▶ Ex. 1

Some nouns are countable.
   a book → **two** books   **an** egg → **six** eggs
Some nouns are uncountable.
   bread   rice
Some nouns are both!
   Do you like **coffee**?   We'd like three **coffees**, please.

9.2 *would like* ▶ Ex. 2

Would is the same in all persons.
We use *would like* in offers and requests.

Affirmative

I You He/She/It We They	'd like	a drink.	'd = would

Yes/No questions

Would	you he/she/it they	like a cookie?

Short answers

Yes, please.
No, thank you.

9.3 *some* and *any* ▶ Ex. 3–4

We use *some* in affirmative sentences with noncount nouns and plural nouns.

There is	some	bread	on the table.
There are		oranges	

We use *some* in questions when we ask for things and offer things.

Can I have	some	coffee, please?
Would you like		grapes?

We use *any* in questions and negative sentences with noncount nouns and plural nouns.

Is there	any	water?
Does she have		children?
I can't see		rice.
There aren't		people.

(I don't know if there is any water. I don't know if she has any children.)

9.4 *How much ... ?* and *How many ... ?* ▶ Ex. 4

We use *How much ... ?* with noncount nouns.
   How much rice is there?   There isn't much rice.
We use *How many ... ?* with count nouns.
   How many apples are there?   There aren't many apples.

9.5 Prepositions

I have a book **by** John Grisham.
What did you have **for** breakfast?

EXERCISES

1 Write C (count) or N (noncount).
1. milk — *N*
2. money — *N*
3. homework — *C*
4. CD — *C*
5. apple — *C*
6. bread — *N*
7. fruit — *N*
8. tea — *N*

2 Complete the sentences. Use *Would ... like* or *'d like*.
1. I *'d like* a cup of coffee, please.
2. *like* they *'d like* some food?
3. *like* you *'d like* to go out tonight?
4. *like* she *like* a drink?

3 Choose the correct word.
1. Can I have *any / some* milk, please?
2. Do they have *some / any* sandwiches?
3. There are *some / any* oranges.
4. Would you like *any / some* coffee?
5. Are there *any / some* cookies?

4 Complete the sentences. Use *is, are, some, any, much,* or *many*.
1. How *much* sugar is there?
2. I'd like *many* water, please.
3. *some* there any bread?
4. How *any* people did you see?
5. There *are* some letters for you.
6. Do you have *is* money?

UNIT 10

10.1 Present Continuous ▶ Ex. 1–2

1. The Present Continuous describes an activity that is happening now.
   > She**'s wearing** jeans.
   > I**'m studying** English.

2. It also describes an activity in the near future.
   > I**'m playing** tennis this afternoon.
   > Jane**'s going** to a party tonight.

Affirmative and negative

I	am		
He She It	is	(not) going	outside.
We You They	are		

Question

Where	am	I	
	is	he she it	going?
	are	we you they	

Yes/No questions	Short answers
Are you having a good time?	Yes, we are.
Is my English getting better?	Yes, it is.
Are they having a party?	No, they aren't.

Spelling of verb + -ing

1. Most verbs just add -ing.
   > wear → wear**ing**   go → go**ing**   cook → cook**ing**

2. If the infinitive ends in -e, drop the -e.
   > write → wri**ting**   smile → smi**ling**

3. When a one-syllable verb has one vowel and ends in a consonant, double the consonant.
   > sit → si**tting**   get → ge**tting**   run → ru**nning**

10.2 Present Simple and Present Continuous ▶ Ex. 3

1. The Present Simple describes things that are always true, or true for a long time.
   > I **come** from Taiwan.
   > He **works** in a bank.

2. The Present Continuous describes activities happening now, and temporary activities.
   > Why **are you wearing** a suit? You usually wear jeans.

10.3 *Whose* + possessive pronouns ▶ Ex. 4

Whose ...? asks about possession.

Subject	Object	Adjective	Pronoun
I	me	my	mine
You	you	your	yours
He	him	his	his
She	her	her	hers
We	us	our	ours
They	them	their	theirs

Whose is this book? Whose book is this? Whose is it?	It's	mine. yours. hers. his. ours. theirs.

10.4 Prepositions

We have this sweater **in** red.
He's talking **to** Mandy.
There's a girl **with** blonde hair.
I'm looking **for** a sweater.
I always pay **by** credit card.

EXERCISES

1 Complete the sentences. Use the Present Continuous.
1. He _____ math at the university. (study)
2. I _____ away this weekend. (not go)
3. _____ they _____ ? (work)
4. She _____ the party. (not enjoy)
5. _____ you _____ Sam tonight? (see)

2 Write the -*ing* form.
1. write _____
2. stop _____
3. wear _____
4. go _____
5. dance _____

3 Complete the sentences. Use the Present Simple or Continuous.
1. Juan _____ from San Jose. (come)
2. I _____ Jo at 6 P.M. tonight. (meet)
3. Why _____ you _____ now? (laugh)
4. She always _____ nice clothes. (wear)
5. We're late! _____ you _____ ? (come)

4 Complete the sentences. Use *Whose* or *Who's*.
1. _____ books are these?
2. _____ standing at the door?
3. _____ going to pass the exam?
4. _____ pen is this?
5. _____ dog is that?

11.1 *going to* ▶ Ex. 1

1. *Going to* expresses a person's plans and intentions.

    She's **going to** be a ballet dancer when she grows up.
    We're **going to** stay in a villa in France this summer.

2. Often there is no difference between *going to* and the Present Continuous to refer to a future intention.

    I'm seeing Peter tonight.
    I'm going to see Peter tonight.

3. We also use *going to* when we can see now that something is sure to happen in the future.

    Careful! That glass is **going to** fall!

Affirmative and negative

I	am		
He/She/It	is	(not) going to	take a break.
We/You/They	are		stay at home.

Questions

	am	I		
When	is	he/she/it	going to	take a break?
	are	we/you/they		stay at home?

With the verbs *to go* and *to come*, we usually use the Present Continuous for future plans.

    We're **going** to San Francisco next week.
    Joe and Tim **are coming** for lunch tomorrow.

11.2 Comparative and superlative adjectives ▶ Ex. 2–3

	Adjective	Comparative	Superlative
One-syllable adjectives	old	old**er**	the old**est**
	safe	safe**r**	the safe**st**
	big	big**ger***	the big**gest***
	hot	hot**ter***	the hot**test***
Adjectives ending in -*y*	noisy	nois**ier**	the nois**iest**
	dirty	dirt**ier**	the dirt**iest**
Two or more syllable adjectives	boring	**more** boring	the **most** boring
	beautiful	**more** beautiful	the **most** beautiful
Irregular adjectives	good	**better**	the **best**
	bad	**worse**	the **worst**
	far	**farther**	the **farthest**

* Adjectives that end in one vowel and one consonant double the consonant.

    You're **older than** me.
    New York is **dirtier than** Seoul.
    Kyoto is one of **the most beautiful** cities in Asia.

11.3 Prepositions

What did he do **as** a child?
He grew up **in** the city.

What's **on** TV tonight?
I'm going **to** Florida **in** a year.

1 Complete the sentences. Use *going to* (+, – , or ?).

1. (+) Look! It _____ be a nice day!
2. (?) _____ Bill _____ see Dan tonight?
3. (–) I _____ study this weekend.
4. (+) Be careful! You _____ fall.
5. (–) We _____ play football today.
6. (?) _____ you _____ cook dinner tonight?
7. (+) He _____ pass the exam.
8. (–) I _____ work tomorrow.
9. (?) _____ they _____ stay with us?

2 Write the comparative and superlative form.

1. easy _____ → _____
2. boring _____ → _____
3. far _____ → _____
4. noisy _____ → _____
5. nice _____ → _____

3 Put a check next to the correct sentence in each pair.

1. ☐ My computer's bigger than yours.
   ☐ My computer is more big than yours.

2. ☐ This is the noisyest city I know!
   ☐ This is the noisiest city I know!

3. ☐ It's the worse movie in the world.
   ☐ It's the worst movie in the world.

4. ☐ Miami is hotter than Atlanta.
   ☐ Miami is hoter than Atlanta.

5. ☐ Museums are boringer than parks.
   ☐ Museums are more boring than parks.

12.1 Present Perfect ▶ Ex. 1–4

1. The Present Perfect refers to an action that happened some time before now.

    She**'s traveled** to most parts of the world.
    Have you ever **been** in a car accident?

2. If we want to say *when* these actions happened, we must use the Past Simple.

    She **went** to Singapore two years ago.
    I **was** in a crash when I was 10.

3. Notice the time expressions used with the Past Simple.

I left	last night/yesterday/in 1990/at three o'clock/on Monday.

Affirmative and negative

I You We They	have	(not) been	to Canada.
He She It	has		

I've been = I have been
You've been = You have been
We've been = We have been
They've been = They have been

He's been = He has been
She's been = She has been
It's been = It has been

been and gone

She's **gone** to Korea. (= she's there now)
She's **been** to Korea. (= now she has returned)

Question

Where	have	I you we they	been?
	has	she he it	

Yes/No questions
Have you been to Colombia?

Short answers
Yes, I have./No, I haven't.

ever and never

We use *ever* in questions and *never* in negative sentences.

    Have you **ever** been to Colombia?
    I've **never** been to Colombia.

12.2 yet ▶ Ex. 3

We use *yet* in negative sentences and questions.

    Have you done your homework **yet**?
    I haven't done it **yet** (but I'm going to).

12.3 Prepositions

She works **for** a big company.
Ryan and Tara are **on** their honeymoon.
Hamlet is a play **by** Shakespeare.

EXERCISES

1 Put a check next to the correct sentence in each pair.

1. ☐ I went to Tokyo last year.
   ☐ I have been to Tokyo last year.

2. ☐ Have you ever met a famous person?
   ☐ Did you ever meet a famous person?

3. ☐ Kate's not here. She's been to Boston.
   ☐ Kate's not here. She's gone to Boston.

4. ☐ You have met him when you were six.
   ☐ You met him when you were six.

2 Complete the sentences. Use the Present Perfect (+, –, or ?).

1. (+) He _____ all over the world. (travel)
2. (?) _____ you ever _____ this movie? (see)
3. (–) We _____ on vacation this year. (be)
4. (+) They _____ your letter. (read)
5. (?) _____ Bill _____ the laundry? (do)
6. (–) We _____ the card yet. (send)

3 Put the adverb in the correct place.

1. Have you finished the report? (yet) _____
2. I've been to Australia. (never) _____
3. Has Tony lived in New York? (ever) _____

4 Write short answers that are true for you.

1. Have you ever been to Taiwan? _____
2. Have you taken any exams this year? _____
3. Have any of your friends ever played in a rock band? _____
4. Has your best friend ever lied to you? _____
5. Has the class ended yet? _____

Pairwork Activities Student A

UNIT 8 page 56

Famous inventions

When were things invented? With a partner, ask and answer questions.

When was Coca-Cola invented?

In 1886.

That's . . . years ago.

1. Coca-Cola was invented in _____ .
2. The camera was invented in __1826__ .
3. The record player was invented in _____ .
4. The first plane was invented in __1903__ .
5. Jeans were invented in _____ .
6. Hamburgers were invented in __1895__ .
7. Cars were invented in _____ .
8. The telephone was invented in __1876__ .
9. The television was invented in _____ .
10. Bicycles were invented in about __1840__ .

UNIT 8 page 58

Did you know that?

With a partner, make similar conversations.

A Did you know that Marco Polo brought spaghetti back from China?
B Really? That's incredible!
A Well, it's true.
B Did you know that Napoleon was afraid of cats?
A No way! I don't believe it!
B Well, it's true!

Did you know that ...

... Vincent van Gogh sold only two of his paintings while he was alive?
... American TV talk show host Oprah Winfrey could read before she was three?
... Shakespeare spelled his name in eleven different ways?
... in 1979 it snowed in the Sahara desert?
... King Louis XIV of France took a bath only three times in his life?

UNIT 10 page 72

Who's at the party?

Work with a partner. You each have a picture of a party. Talk about the pictures to find ten differences. *Don't* show your picture to your partner!

In my picture three people are dancing.

In my picture four people are dancing.

There's a woman with brown hair.

Is she wearing a black dress?

Pairwork Activities Student B

UNIT 8 *page 56*

Famous inventions

When were things invented? With a partner, ask and answer questions.

When was the camera invented?

In 1826.

That's . . . years ago.

1. Coca-Cola was invented in __1886__ .
2. The camera was invented in _____ .
3. The record player was invented in __1878__ .
4. The first plane was invented in _____ .
5. Jeans were invented in __1873__ .
6. Hamburgers were invented in _____ .
7. Cars were invented in __1893__ .
8. The telephone was invented in _____ .
9. The television was invented in __1926__ .
10. Bicycles were invented in about _____ .

UNIT 8 *page 58* Did you know that?

Did you know that?

With a partner, make similar conversations.

> **A** Did you know that Marco Polo brought spaghetti back from China?
> **B** Really? That's incredible!
> **A** Well, it's true.
> **B** Did you know that Napoleon was afraid of cats?
> **A** No way! I don't believe it!
> **B** Well, it's true!

Did you know that ...

... it took 1,700 years to build the Great Wall of China?
... Walt Disney used his own voice for the character of Mickey Mouse?
... Shakespeare and Cervantes both died on April 23, 1616?
... King Francis I of France bought the painting *Mona Lisa* to put in his bathroom?
... when Shakespeare was alive, there were no actresses, only male actors?

UNIT 10 *page 72*

Who's at the party?

Work with a partner. You each have a picture of a party. Talk about the pictures to find ten differences. *Don't* show your picture to your partner!

In my picture three people are dancing.

In my picture four people are dancing.

There's a woman with brown hair.

Is she wearing a black dress?

UNIT 11 *page 84*

The weather

Work with a partner. Find out about the weather around the world yesterday. Look at the information on this page. Ask and answer questions to complete the information.

What was the weather like in Atlanta?

It was sunny and hot. Eighty-six degrees.

WORLD WEATHER NOON YESTERDAY

		°F			°F
Atlanta	S	86	Mexico City	S	77
Boston	C	65	San Francisco		
Brasilia			São Paulo	S	77
Denver	C	60	Seattle		
Hong Kong			Toronto	C	60
London	Fg	59	Vancouver		
Los Angeles					

S = sunny
C = cloudy
Fg = foggy
R = rainy
Sn = snowy

Word List

UNIT 7

act *v* /ækt/
activity *n* /æk'tɪvəti/
airplane *n* /'ɛrpleɪn/
after that *adv* /'æftər 'ðæt/
agree *v* /ə'gri/
air show *n* /ɛr ʃoʊ/
another *pron* /ə'nʌðər/
April *n* /'eɪprəl/
astronaut *n* /'æstrənɔt/
at that moment /ət 'ðæt 'moʊmənt/
athlete *n* /'æθlit/
Atlantic *n* /ət'læntɪk/
become *v* /bɪ'kʌm/
begin *v* /bɪ'gɪn/
birthday *n* /'bərθdeɪ/
break a record /breɪk eɪ 'rɛkərd/
crash *n* /kræʃ/
career *n* /kə'rɪr/
century *n* /'sɛntʃəri/
champion *n* /'tʃæmpiən/
change *v* /tʃeɪndʒ/
Christmas Day *n* /ˌkrɪsməs 'deɪ/
Congratulations!
    /kəngrætʃə'leɪʃnz/
countryside *n* /'kʌntrɪsaɪd/
dangerous *adj* /'deɪndʒərəs/
decide *v* /dɪ'saɪd/
die *v* /daɪ/
disappear *v* /dɪsə'pɪr/
earn *v* /ərn/
end *n, v* /ɛnd/
Europe *n* /'yʊərəp/
everybody *pron* /'ɛvribadi/
excellent *adj* /'ɛksələnt/
experience *n* /ɪk'spɪriəns/
famous *adj* /'feɪməs/
farm *n* /farm/
fighter jet *n* /'faɪtər dʒɛt/
movie star *n* /'muvi star/
film studio *n* /fɪlm 'studioʊ/
finally *adv* /'faɪnli/
first (... next) *adv* /fərst/

flight *n* /'flaɪt/
foreign minister *n* /'fɔrən 'mɪnəstər/
fortunately *adv* /'fɔrtʃənətli/
guitar *n* /gɪtar/
handbag *n* /'hændbæg/
immediately *adv* /ɪ'midiətli/
important *adj* /ɪm'pɔrtnt/
Independence Day *n* /ɪndɪ'pɛndəns ˌdeɪ/
join *v* /dʒɔɪn/
June *n* /dʒun/
later *adv* /leɪtər/
leader *n* /'lidər/
leave *v* /liv/
life *n* /laɪf/
march *n* /martʃ/
marry *v* /'mæri/
meal *n* /mil/
medal *n* /'mɛdl/
million *n* /'mɪlyən/
money *n* /'mʌni/
Mother's Day *n* /'mʌðərz ˌdeɪ/
nearly *adv* /'nɪrli/
news *n* /nuz/
November *n* /noʊ'vɛmbər/
olympics *n* /ə'lɪmpɪks/
over *prep* /'oʊvər/
orange juice *n* /'ɔrɪndʒ dʒus/
own *v* /oʊn/
Pacific Ocean *n* /pəˌsɪfɪk 'oʊʃn/
parking lot *n* /'parkɪŋ lat/
personal computer *n* /'pərsənl kəm'pyutər/
pilot *n* /'paɪlət/
politician *n* /palə'tɪʃn/
politics *n* /'palətɪks/
popular *adj* /'papyələr/
present (= birthday) *n* /'prɛznt/
president *n* /'prɛzədənt/
public *n* /'pʌblɪk/
remember *v* /rɪ'mɛmbər/
retire *v* /rɪ'taɪər/
rich *adj* /rɪtʃ/
satellite *n* /'sætlaɪt/
secret *adj* /'sikrət/
sell *v* /sɛl/
September *n* /sɛp'tɛmbər/
shoes *n* /ʃuz/
short *adj* /ʃɔrt/
sleep *v* /slip/
soon *adv* /sun/
space *n* /speɪs/
star *n* /star/
study *v* /'stʌdi/
subject (school) *n* /'sʌbdʒɛkt/
sure *adj* /ʃʊr/
survive *v* /sər'vaɪv/
take a vacation *v* /teɪk eɪ veɪ'keɪʃn/
temple *n* /'tɛmpl/
test flight *n* /'tɛst flaɪt/
test pilot *n* /'tɛst paɪlət/
thank goodness /ˌθæŋk 'gʊdnəs/
think *v* /θɪŋk/
tomorrow *adv* /tə'maroʊ/
war *n* /wɔr/
win *v* /wɪn/

UNIT 8

advice *v* /əd'vaɪs/
afraid *adj* /ə'freɪd/
(3 years) ago *adv* /ə'goʊ/
all the time *adv* /ˌɔl ðə 'taɪm/
arrive *v* /ə'raɪv/
(coffee) break *n* /breɪk/
bicycle *n* (bike) / 'baɪsɪkl/
birthday *n* /'bərθdeɪ/
call *v* /kɔl/
Christmas Day *n* /ˌkrɪsməs 'deɪ/
couple *n pl* /'kʌpl/
cry *v* /kraɪ/
date *n* /deɪt/
design *n* /dɪ'zaɪn/
driver *n* /'draɪvər/
easy *adj* /'izi/
Easter Day *n* /'istər 'deɪ/
everyone *n* /'ɛvriwʌn/
experiment *n* /ɪk'spɛrəmənt/
fall *n* *US* (autumn) / fɔl/
fall in love *v* /fɔl ɪn lʌv/
feelings *n pl* /'filɪŋz/
forget *v* /fər'gɛt/
get engaged *v* /ˌgɛt ɪn'geɪdʒd/
get married *v* /ˌgɛt 'mærɪd/
give *v* /gɪv/
Good luck! /ˌgʊd 'lʌk/
government *n* /'gʌvərmənt/
green *adj* /grin/
Halloween *n* /ˌhælə'win/
horse *n* /hɔrs/
idea *n* /aɪ'diə/
in a hurry /ˌɪn ər 'həri/
incredible *adj* /ɪn'krɛdəbl/
inside *prep* /ɪn'saɪd/
invent *v* /ɪn'vɛnt/
invention *n* /ɪn'vɛnʃn/
invitation *n* /ɪnvə'teɪʃn/
jeans *n pl* /dʒinz/
laugh *v* /læf/
long ago *adv* /lɔŋ ə'goʊ/
midnight *n* /'mɪdnaɪt/
mistake *n* /mɪ'steɪk/
Mother's Day *n* /'mʌðərz deɪ/
New Year's Eve *n* /nu yɪrz iv/
notice *v* /'noʊtəs/
nowadays *adv* /'naʊədeɪz/
opera *n* /'aprə/
painter *n* /'peɪntər/
phone call *n* /foʊn ˌkɔl/
same to you /seɪm tə yu/
semester *n* /sə'mɛstər/
send *v* /sɛnd/
snow *n* /snoʊ/
spaghetti *n* /spə'gɛti/
studio *n* /'studioʊ/
sweet *adj* /'swɪt/
Thanksgiving *n* /θæŋks'gɪvɪŋ/
tomorrow *n* /tə'maroʊ/
type *n, v* /taɪp/
unhappy *adj* /ʌn'hæpi/

Valentine's Day n /'væləntaɪnz deɪ/
wedding day n /'wɛdɪŋ deɪ/
windshield wiper n /'wɪndʃild 'waɪpər/

UNIT 9

all sorts n pl /'ɔl sɔrts/
anybody pron /'ɛnibʌdi/
anything else? /'ɛniθɪŋ ɛls/
anyway adv /'ɛniweɪ/
apple juice n /'æpl dʒus/
away from adv /ə'weɪ frəm/
bacon n /'beɪkən/
banana n /bə'nænə/
beef n /bif/
book v /bʊk/
borrow v /'baroʊ/
bottle n /'batl/
box n /baks/
bread n /brɛd/
carrot n /'kærət/
central adj /'sɛntrəl/
check in/out v /tʃɛk 'ɪn/'aʊt/
cheese n /tʃiz/
chicken n /'tʃɪkən/
Chile n /'tʃɪli/
chili n /'tʃɪli/
China n /'tʃaɪnə/
Chinese adj /tʃaɪ'niz/
chocolate n /'tʃaklət/
chopsticks n pl /'tʃapstɪks/
close v /kloʊs/
coffee n /'kɔfi/
control v /kən'troʊl/
cookie n /'kʊki/
course (of a meal) n /kɔrs/
cream n /krim/
delicious adj /dɪ'lɪʃəs/
depend v /dɪ'pɛnd/
dessert n /dɪ'zərt/
disgusting adj /dɪs'gʌstɪŋ/
dollar n /'dalər/
double room n /,dʌbl 'rʊm/
egg n /ɛg/
either adv /'iðər/
environment n /ɛn'vaɪərnmənt/
especially adv /ɪ'spɛʃəli/
farm v /farm/
finger n /'fɪŋgər/
fish n /fɪʃ/
for example /,fər ɪg'zæmpl/
foreign adj /'fɔrən/
fruit n /frut/
full adj /fʊl/
garlic n /'garlɪk/
glad adj /glæd/
history n /'hɪstri/
homework n /'hoʊmwərk/
horrible adj /'hɔrəbl/
human adj /'hyumən/
hungry adj /'hʌngri/
land n /lænd/
lend v /lɛnd/
lunch n /lʌntʃ/
main (meal) adj /meɪn/
meat n /mit/
menu n /'mɛnyu/

(the) Middle East n /(ðə) ,mɪdl 'ist/
milk n /mɪlk/
move on v /muv 'an/
mushroom n /'mʌʃrum/
noodles n pl /'nudlz/
north n /nɔrθ/
orange n /'ɔrɪndʒ/
part (of the world) n /part/
pass (= give) v /pæs/
pasta n /'pastə/
pea n /pi/
pancakes n /'pænkeɪks/
poor adj /pʊr/
possible adj /'pasəbl/
potatoes n pl /pə'teɪtoʊz/
pound n, v /paʊnd/
recipe n /'rɛsəpi/
rice n /raɪs/
right now adv /,raɪt 'naʊ/
salt n /sɔlt/
seafood n /'sifud/
shopping list n /ʃapɪŋ ,lɪst/
single room n /,sɪŋgl 'rʊm/
soda n /'soʊdə/
south n /saʊθ/
bottled water n /'batld 'wɔtər/
tap water n /tæp 'wɔtər/
strawberry n /'strɔbɛri/
sugar n /'ʃʊgər/
table n /'teɪbl/
Taiwanese adj /taɪwɑ'niz/
tea n /ti/
Thailand n /'taɪlænd/
toast n /toʊst/
together adv /tə'gɛðər/
tomato n /tə'meɪtoʊ/
transport v /træn'spɔrt/
tuna n /'tunə/
typical adj /'tɪpɪkl/
vegetable n /'vɛdʒtəbl/
yogurt n /'yoʊgərt/
yours faithfully /yərz 'feɪθflɪ/

UNIT 10

backyard n /bæk'yard/
baseball cap n /'beɪsbɔl ,kæp/
bicycle n /'baɪsɪkl/
blonde n, adj /bland/
fitting rooms n pl /'fɪtɪŋ rʊmz/
cherish v /'tʃɛrɪʃ/
chewing gum n /'tʃuɪŋ ,gʌm/
choose v /tʃuz/
coat n /koʊt/
credit card n /'krɛdət kard/
dark adj /dark/
deny v /dɪ'naɪ/
dog n /dɔg/
dress n /drɛs/
flowers n /flaʊərs/
fresh adj /frɛʃ/
good-looking adj /,gʊd'lʊkɪŋ/
gray n, adj /greɪ/
hair n /hɛr/
handsome adj /'hænsəm/
happiness n /'hæpinəs/

hat n /hæt/
jacket n /'dʒækət/
joy n /dʒɔɪ/
kiss v /kɪs/
long adj /lɔŋ/
pants n /pænts/
pay v /peɪ/
shirt n /ʃərt/
shoe n /ʃu/
shorts n pl /ʃɔrts/
size n /saɪz/
skateboard n /'skeɪtbɔrd/
skirt n /skərt/
smile v /smaɪl/
sneakers n /'snikərs/
soccer ball n /'sakər bɔl/
solitary adj /'salətɛri/
something n /'sʌmθɪŋ/
suit n /sut/
suitcase n /'sutkeɪs/
sunglasses n pl /'sʌnglæsəs/
sunrise n /'sʌnraɪz/
sweater n /'swɛtər/
T-shirt n /'tiʃərt/
talk v /tɔk/
tennis racket n /'tɛnəs 'rækət/
try on v /,traɪ an/
umbrella n /ʌm'brɛlə/
whose? pron /huz/
wing n /wɪŋ/

UNIT 11

adventure n /əd'vɛntʃər/
art n /art/
bathing suit n /bæθɪŋ sut/
bottom n /batəm/
breath n /brɛθ/
breathe v /brið/
calm adj /kam/
catch (a bus) v /kætʃ/
climb v /klaɪm/
cloudy adj /'klaʊdi/
continue v /kən'tɪnyu/
cool adj /kul/
conservation n /kansər'veɪʃn/
(18) degrees n pl /dɪ'griz/
deep adj /dip/
discover v /dɪs'kʌvər/
drive v /draɪv/
due (a baby) adj /du/
fall v /fɔl/
foggy adj /'fɔgi/
free diving n /'fri daɪvɪŋ/
free running n /'fri rʌnɪŋ/
freedom n /'fridəm/
grow up v /,groʊ 'ʌp/
gymnastics n /dʒɪm'næstɪks/
join v /dʒɔɪn/
jump v /dʒʌmp/
lion n /'laɪən/
meeting n /'mitɪŋ/
meter n /'mitər/
move n /muv/
outside prep /'aʊtsaɪd/
oxygen n /'aksɪdʒən/
pain n /peɪn/

peace *n* /pis/
philosophy *n* /fə'lɑsəfi/
plan *n, v* /plæn/
quiet *adj* /'kwaɪət/
rainforest *n* /reɪnfɔrəst/
retire *v* /rɪ'taɪər/
roof *n* /ruf/
safe *adj* /seɪf/
scuba dive *v* /'skubədaɪv/
sneeze *v* /sniz/
snowy *adj* /'snoʊi/
stay *v* /steɪ/
suggestion *n* /səg'dʒɛstʃən/
try *v* /traɪ/
umbrella *n* /ʌm'brɛlə/
underwater *adj, adv*
    /ʌndər'wɔtər/
view *n* /vyu/
weather *n* /'wɛðər/
windy *adj* /'wɪndi/

monitor *n, v* /'mɑnətər/
motorcycle *n* /moʊtərsaɪkl/
now boarding /ˌnaʊ bɔrdɪŋ/
pack (a bag) *v* /pæk/
passenger *n* /'pæsɪndʒər/
passport control *n* /'pæsport kən'troʊl/
elementary school *n*
    /'ɛlə'mɛntəri skul/
(the) Pyramids *n pl* /ðə 'pɪrəmɪdz/
quarrel *n* /'kwɔrəl/
reason *n* /'rizn/
retired *adj* /rɪ'taɪərd/
seat *n* /sit/
stay *v* /steɪ/
three-course (meal) *n* /ˌθri kɔrs 'mil/
tornado *n* /tɔr'neɪdoʊ/
waste (of time) *v* /'weɪst/

UNIT 12

abroad *adv* /ə'brɔd/
airport *n* /'ɛrpɔrt/
attack *v* /ə'tæk/
announcement *n* /ə'naʊnsmənt/
arrival area *n* /ə'raɪvl 'ɛriə/
board *v* /bɔrd/
boarding pass *n* /bɔrdɪŋ pæs/
boat ride *n* /'boʊt ˌraɪd/
business class *n* /'bɪznəs klæs/
cart *n, v* /kɑrt/
carry-on luggage *n* /'kæri ɑn 'lʌgɪdʒ/
check in *v* /tʃɛk ɪn/
check-in counter *n* /tʃɛk ɪn 'kaʊntər/
comfort *n* /'kʌmfərt/
competition *n* /kɑmpə'tɪʃn/
cycle *v* /'saɪkl/
deliver *v* /dɪ'lɪvər/
departure gate *n* /dɪ'pɑrtʃər ˌgeɪt/
departure lounge *n* /dɪ'pɑrtʃər ˌlaʊndʒ/
excellent *adj* /'ɛksələnt/
execute *v* /'ɛksəkyut/
flag *n* /flæg/
flight *n* /flaɪt/
fly *v* /flaɪ/
gate (in an airport) *n* /geɪt/
(the) Government *n* /'gʌərmənt/
hand luggage *n* /'hænd ˌlʌgɪdʒ/
hearse *n* /hərs/
hitchhike *v* /'hɪtʃˌhaɪk/
honeymoon *n* /'hʌnimun/
horse and cart *n* /hɔrs ənd kɑrt/
hurt *v* /hərt/
jumbo jet *n* /'dʒʌmboʊ dʒɛt/
kill *v* /kɪl/
knee *n* /ni/
last call *n* /ˌlæst 'kɔl/
lie *v* /laɪ/
lift *n* /lɪft/
locust *n* /loʊkəst/
loud *adj* /laʊd/
luggage *n* /'lʌgɪdʒ/
mad *adj* /mæd/
miss *v* /mɪs/

Irregular Verbs

Base form	Past Simple	Past participle
be	was/were	been
become	became	become
begin	began	begun
break	broke	broken
bring	brought	brought
build	built	built
buy	bought	bought
can	could	been able
catch	caught	caught
choose	chose	chosen
come	came	come
cost	cost	cost
cut	cut	cut
do	did	done
drink	drank	drunk
drive	drove	driven
eat	ate	eaten
fall	fell	fallen
feel	felt	felt
fight	fought	fought
find	found	found
fly	flew	flown
forget	forgot	forgotten
get	got	gotten
give	gave	given
go	went	gone/been
grow	grew	grown
have	had	had
hear	heard	heard
hit	hit	hit
keep	kept	kept
know	knew	known
leave	left	left
lose	lost	lost
make	made	made
meet	met	met
pay	paid	paid
put	put	put
read /rid/	read /rɛd/	read /rɛd/
ride	rode	ridden
run	ran	run
say	said	said
see	saw	seen
sell	sold	sold
send	sent	sent
shut	shut	shut
sing	sang	sung
sit	sat	sat
sleep	slept	slept
speak	spoke	spoken
spend	spent	spent
stand	stood	stood
steal	stole	stolen
swim	swam	swum
take	took	taken
tell	told	told
think	thought	thought
understand	understood	understood
wake	woke	woken
wear	wore	worn
win	won	won
write	wrote	written

Verb Patterns

Verb + -ing

like love enjoy hate finish stop	swimming cooking

Verb + to + infinitive

choose decide forget manage promise need help hope try want would like would love	to go to work

Verb + -ing or to + infinitive

begin start	raining/to rain

Modal auxiliary verbs

can could will would	go arrive

Phonetic Symbols

Consonants			
1	/p/	as in	**pen** /pɛn/
2	/b/	as in	**big** /bɪg/
3	/t/	as in	**tea** /ti/
4	/d/	as in	**do** /du/
5	/k/	as in	**cat** /kæt/
6	/g/	as in	**go** /goʊ/
7	/f/	as in	**five** /faɪv/
8	/v/	as in	**very** /ˈvɛri/
9	/s/	as in	**son** /sʌn/
10	/z/	as in	**zoo** /zu/
11	/l/	as in	**live** /lɪv/
12	/m/	as in	**my** /maɪ/
13	/n/	as in	**nine** /naɪn/
14	/h/	as in	**happy** /ˈhæpi/
15	/r/	as in	**red** /rɛd/
16	/y/	as in	**yes** /yɛs/
17	/w/	as in	**want** /wɒnt/
18	/θ/	as in	**thanks** /θæŋks/
19	/ð/	as in	**the** /ðə/
20	/ʃ/	as in	**she** /ʃi/
21	/ʒ/	as in	**television** /ˈtɛlɪvɪʒn/
22	/tʃ/	as in	**child** /tʃaɪld/
23	/dʒ/	as in	**Japan** /dʒəˈpæn/
24	/ŋ/	as in	**English** /ˈɪŋglɪʃ/

Vowels			
25	/i/	as in	**see** /si/
26	/ɪ/	as in	**his** /hɪz/
27	/ɛ/	as in	**ten** /tɛn/
28	/æ/	as in	**stamp** /stæmp/
29	/ɑ/	as in	**father** /ˈfɑðər/
30	/ɔ/	as in	**saw** /sɔ/
31	/ʊ/	as in	**book** /bʊk/
32	/u/	as in	**you** /yu/
33	/ʌ/	as in	**sun** /sʌn/
34	/ə/	as in	**about** /əˈbaʊt/
35	/eɪ/	as in	**name** /neɪm/
36	/aɪ/	as in	**my** /maɪ/
37	/ɔɪ/	as in	**boy** /bɔɪ/
38	/aʊ/	as in	**how** /haʊ/
39	/oʊ/	as in	**go** /goʊ/
40	/ər/	as in	**bird** /bərd/
41	/ɪr/	as in	**near** /nɪr/
42	/ɛr/	as in	**hair** /hɛr/
43	/ar/	as in	**car** /kar/
44	/ɔr/	as in	**more** /mɔr/
45	/ʊr/	as in	**tour** /tʊr/

OXFORD
UNIVERSITY PRESS

198 Madison Avenue
New York, NY 10016 USA

Great Clarendon Street, Oxford OX2 6DP UK

Oxford University Press is a department of the University of Oxford.
It furthers the University's objective of excellence in research, scholarship,
and education by publishing worldwide in

Oxford   New York

Auckland   Cape Town   Dar es Salaam   Hong Kong   Karachi
Kuala Lumpur   Madrid   Melbourne   Mexico City   Nairobi
New Delhi   Shanghai   Taipei   Toronto

With offices in

Argentina   Austria   Brazil   Chile   Czech Republic   France   Greece
Guatemala   Hungary   Italy   Japan   Poland   Portugal   Singapore
South Korea   Switzerland   Thailand   Turkey   Ukraine   Vietnam

OXFORD and OXFORD ENGLISH are registered trademarks of Oxford University
Press in certain countries.

© Oxford University Press 2009

Database right Oxford University Press (maker)

Editorial Director: Laura Pearson
Publishing Manager: Erik Gundersen
Managing Editor: Louisa van Houten
Development Editor: Rosi Perea
Design Director: Susan Sanguily
Design Manager: Maj-Britt Hagsted
Senior Designer: Michael Steinhofer
Image Editor: Robin Fadool
Design Production Manager: Stephen White
Production Editors: Alissa Heyman, Greg Johnson
Manufacturing Manager: Shanta Persaud
Manufacturing Coordinator: Elizabeth Matsumoto

ISBN Student Book with Multi-ROM (pack): 978-019-472866-9
ISBN Student Book (pack component): 978-019-472753-2
ISBN Multi-ROM (pack component): 978-019-472765-5

Printed in China

10 9 8 7 6 5

This book is printed on paper from certified and well-managed sources.

ACKNOWLEDGEMENTS

Illustrations by: Kathy Baxendale p. 85; Andy Hammond pp. 72, 73, 81; Ned Jolliffe p. 54; Debbie Ryder
p. 92; Gavin Reece p. 71; Barbara Bastian p. 100.

The publishers would like to thank the following for their kind permission to reproduce photographs:
Globe Photos p. 48; Getty Images: Evan Agostini p. 49 (top); Associated Press: Denis Farrell p. 49
(bottom); Woodfin Camp/Aurora Photos/Kainulainen-LEH: pp. 50–51 (fall of the Berlin Wall); Associated
Press: Tsugufumi Matsumoto pp. 50–51 (first Nintendo game); Sipa Press: Carre Christophe pp. 50–51
(Madonna); Corbis: Peter Turnley pp. 50–51 (Mikhail Gorbachev); Corbis p. 52 (Earhart cockpit/Bettmann),
Alamy p. 52 (Gagarin/Popperfoto), Rex Features p. 53 (rocket/ITD), 86 (Westlife/J.Craine), Alamy p. 53
(Earhart standing/Popperfoto), Corbis p. 55 (S.Kennedy), Workbook Stock/Jupiter Images: Nick Daly p. 59
(top right); Popperfoto p. 56 (phone calls), Getty Images p. 56 (cars/Topical Press Agency), Corbis p. 56
(Coca-cola/G.Naylor), Corbis p. 57 (photographs/H.A.Roberts), Corbis p. 56 (television/Hulton-Deutsch
Collection), Popperfoto p. 57 (planes); The Kobal Collection p. 57 (hamburgers/The Advertising Archive
Ltd), The Kobal Collection p. 57 (jeans/The Advertising Archive Ltd); Getty Images p. 57 (bikes/Topical
Press Agency), Corbis p. 57 (records/Hulton-Deutsch Collection), Corbis p. 58 (Macmillan/Hulton-Deutsch
Collection), Getty Images p. 58 (Daguerre/Hulton Archive), Nick Daly p. 59 (top right); Alamy p. 59; (Eric
& Lori/J.Frank), ; Getty Images p. 60 (Easter eggs/G.Gay), Corbis pp. 60–61 (New Year/ Reuters), Corbis
pp. 60–61 (Halloween/A.Skelley), Corbis p. 60 (birthday/N.Schaefer), Getty Images p. 61 (wedding/C.
Havens), p. 61 (Thanksgiving/Photodisc), p. 83 (Naomi/Photodisc), Robert Harding World Imagery p. 61
(Christmas/Digital Vision); Punchstock p. 61 (Mother's Day/ Bananastock), Getty Images p. 62 (Daisy/S.
Biver), Getty Images p. 62 (Piers/ D.Roth); istockphotos: pp. 62–63 (milk); Shutterstock: pp. 62–63 (tea);
istockphotos: pp. 62–63 (French fries); Shutterstock: pp. 62–63 (strawberries); Shutterstock: pp. 62–63
(oranges); Shutterstock: pp. 62–63 (chocolate bar); Shutterstock: pp. 62–63 (carrots); stockexpert.com:
pp. 62–63 (bananas); stockexpert.com pp. 62–63 (cheese); Shutterstock: pp. 62–63 (tomatos); Shutterstock:
pp. 62–63 (soda); StockFood/Getty Images: Lew Robertson pp. 62–63 (fish); istockphoto: pp. 62–63
(bowl of pasta); Shutterstock: pp. 62–63 (peas); Oxford University Press pp. 62–63 (coffee); istockphoto:
pp. 62–63 (apple juice); Workbook Stock/Jupiter Images: Heather Elder pp. 62–63 (pizza); stockexpert.com
pp. 62–63 (cookies); Shutterstock: pp. 62–63 (hamburger); Shutterstock: pp. 62–63 (apples); Shutterstock:
p. 64 (cookies); Anthony Blake Photo Library p. 65 (market/ D.Marsden), FoodPix/Jupiter Images Alan
Richardson p. 68 (Pad Thai); FoodPixJupiter Images: Michael Pohuski p. 68 (American breakfast); Getty
Images pp. 66–67 (Arabs/W.Eastep), Getty Images pp. 66–67 (children eating/D.Sundberg), Lonely Planet
Images pp. 66–67 (noodles/ P.Dymond), Lonely Planet Images pp. 66–67 (truck/D.McKinlay); Alamy
pp. 66–67 (rice harvest/Pictor International), Jupiter Images: p. 71 (child with grandparent); Corbis
pp. 66–67 (salamis/O.Franken), Corbis pp. 66–67 (sardines/J.Van Hasselt), Punchstock p. 66; Getty
Images pp. 66–67 (Sergio/B.Lang), Getty Images pp. 66–67 (Madalena/K.Steele), Getty Images pp. 66–67
(Graham/ S.Joel), Getty Images pp. 66–67 (Anke/M.Krasowitz), Anthony Blake Photo Library pp. 66–67
(Bife/J.Lee Studios), p. 68 (Bruschetta/Foodcollection.com), AsiaPix/Getty Images: p. 68 (Thai male); Stone/
Getty Images: Ron Krisel p. 68 (Italian female); Banana Stock/Jupiter Images: p. 69; Punchstock p. 70
(Alison, Ella & Alfie/Photodisc), p. 70 (Andy/ Photodisc), p. 70 (Poppy/Photodisc), Alamy p. 71 Simon/
Creatas), p. 71 (Colin/Photodisc), p. 71 (Kate & Sofia/Corbis/Digital Stock), Jupiter Images: p. 71 (child
with grandparent); Bananastock/InMagine: p. 75; Getty Images p. 78 (young footballer/Jean Louis Batt/
Photographer's Choice), p. 79 (Punchstock), ,Corbis p. 80 (whale watching/ N.Fobes), Alamy p. 80 (Great
Wall/View Stock China), Alamy p. 80 (Grand Canyon/T.Gervis), Alamy p. 81 (rainforest/ Robert Harding
World Imagery), Alamy p. 81 (lions/T.Manley), Alamy p. 81 (scuba/ G.Bell), Alamy p. 81 (surfing/D.Peebles),
Corbis p. 81 (Everest/R.Holmes), Associated Press p. 82 (Streeter portrait/ H.Cabluck), Associated Press
p. 83 (Streeter diving/P.Shearer); Rex Features p. 83 (Belle portrait/P.Cooper), Rex Features p. 83 (free
running/A.Paradise); Alamy p. 84 (foggy/Imagina/A.Tsunoda), Getty Images p. 85 (umbrellas/Bald Headed
Picture/Taxi), Getty Images p. 85 (couple in rain/Andreas Pollok/Taxi), Getty Images p. 88 (S.Rothfeld),
Moodboard/Alamy: pp. 90–91 (top); Courtesy of Josie Dew: pp. 90–91; Photo Edit Inc.: Kayte M. Deioma
92 (airplane); Punchstock p. 92 (canoeing/Design Pics), Pictures Colour Library p. 92 (Cadre Idris/George
Chetland), Punchstock p. 92 (factory at night/imageshop), Alamy p. 92 (Hyde Park/Alan Copson City
Pictures), Alamy p. 92 (health centre/VIEW Pictures Ltd), Alamy p. 92 (Art museum/Robert Harding
Picture Library), Alamy p. 92 (West End/Alan Copson City Pictures), Alamy p. 92 (Portsmouth/Boating
Images Photo Library), Alamy p. 92 (thatched cottage/Rod Edwards); Getty Images p. 93 (AFP/F.J.Brown),
p. 98 (woman with backpack); p. 98 (temple/Photodisc); Alamy p. 98 (Wales/The Photolibrary Wales),
Alamy p. 99 (girls/ L.Beddoe), Getty Images p. 99 (women/ G.&M.D.de Lossy); Masterfile: Alberto Biscaro
p. 100; Robert Harding/Jupiter Images: Robert Francis p. 102.

Commissioned Photography by: Gareth Boden pp. 58 (Valentine), 77, 88 (Ryan), 98 (Robert), 101; MM Studios
pp. 64–65 (market stall); Ken Karp Photography p. 103.

We are grateful to the following for providing locations: Roberto Gerrards, Hertford & the owner Rob Farrell p. 77;
Photodisc/OUP: p 87.

Cover photos: Pixtal/AGE Fotostock: (top left); Photo Alto/Jupiter Images: James Hardy (top center);
dbimages/Alamy: Roy Johnson (top right); PhotoAlto/AGE Fotostock/: incent Hazat (left center); Masterfile:
(right center); Masterfile: (bottom right); ASP/Getty Images: Kirstin Scholtz (bottom left).

*The authors and publisher are grateful to those who have given permission to reproduce the following extracts and
adaptations of copyright material:* p. 74 'Flying Without Wings' Words & Music by Steve Mac & Wayne Hector
© Copyright 1999 Rokstone Music (50%)/ Rondor Music (London) Limited (50%). All Rights Reserved.
International Copyright Secured. pp. 82–83 Taken from 'The art of Le Parkour' by Hugh Schofield, 19
April 2002, BBC News Online. Reproduced by permission of JP BOSSON Management and the BBC.
pp. 82–83 'Into the deep' by Libby Brooks, 23 July 2003, The Guardian © The Guardian. Reproduced by
permission. pp. 90–91 Taken from Josie Dew's web site www.josiedew.co.uk, 2 April 2004. Reproduced
by permission.